PELICAN BOOKS

Pelican Library of Business and Management

Advisory Editor: T. Kempner

THE EARNINGS CONFLICT

Wilfred Brown is a Scot. After early experience in accountancy and selling in Glasgow he joined the Glacier Metal Co. Ltd in 1931, and was Managing Director and Chairman from 1939 to 1965. In 1964 he became, for one year, a member of the Advisory Council to the Ministry of Technology and was Chairman of the Docks Modernization Committee from 1965 to 1968. From 1965 to 1970 he was Minister of State at the Board of Trade with special responsibility for exports. He became a Member of the Privy Council in 1970, and is Pro-Chancellor of Brunel University. A life peerage was conferred on him in 1964. During the debate on the Industrial Relations Bill he led for the opposition in the House of Lords.

WILFRED BROWN

THE EARNINGS CONFLICT

Proposals for tackling the
emerging crisis of industrial relations,
unemployment, and wage inflation

PENGUIN BOOKS

in association with Heinemann

Penguin Books Ltd, Harmondsworth, Middlesex, England
Penguin Books Inc., 7110 Ambassador Road, Baltimore, Maryland 21207, U.S.A.
Penguin Books Australia Ltd, Ringwood, Victoria, Australia

—

First published by Heinemann Educational Books 1973
Published in Pelican Books 1973

—

Copyright © Wilfred Brown, 1973

—

Made and printed in Great Britain
by Richard Clay (The Chaucer Press) Ltd,
Bungay, Suffolk
Set in Monotype Times

Contents

Acknowledgement

Professor Elliott Jaques of Brunel University originally proposed that we should write this book as a joint endeavour. But heavy engagement in research, particularly into the organization of the National Health Service, deprived him of the necessary time. We therefore agreed that I should write it alone.

The Earnings Conflict Film

The proposed institution (NCRD) for dealing with National Wages Differentials, described in this book, is discussed in a 25 minute 16mm colour film. This film is now available for purchase or hire from Cygnet Films Ltd., Bushey Studio, Melbourne Road, Bushey, Herts. Tel. 01–950 1621.

CHAPTER 1

The essential conditions for satisfactory employment

More than ninety per cent of the working population in Britain today are employees. Less than five per cent are either employers or self-employed. Nearly twenty-three million people spend a major portion of their lives at paid work. The environment of work and all that happens within it plays a very large part in conditioning our entire psychological response to living. If we enjoy work we have a better chance of enjoying the other parts of our lives. If we resent the conditions of employment and fail to get any kick out of our daily work, then we may find compensation in other ways but unsatisfactory employment may cast a shadow on everything we do.

This book is about employment and the widespread belief in society that work in employment is becoming increasingly less satisfying to the majority of people.

The current pessimism about employment

There is a widespread opinion that the smaller the company the happier the conditions of work. As in fact the average size of companies is constantly increasing this may be a significant factor. Many people believe that dissatisfaction at work is caused by increasing mechanization and computerization. Certainly these trends do, in the short term, tend to deprive many people of work which involved their full capabilities. But in the long run all forms of automation reduce the proportion of very simple jobs and increase the number of complex jobs. Nevertheless there is currently a general feeling of pessimism about the employment situation. People say that employment is a rat-race and will continue to be a rat-race; that advancing technology will condemn more and more people to deadening boredom or worse, unemployment; that the clash between management and labour is inevitable; and that the highest rewards will always go to the slick or the bellicose.

7

But this is not a pessimistic book. I believe that society has, within its power, the ability to make employment different. *My object is to try to give as many people as possible the conviction that the problem can be tackled. I want to dispel the pervading assumption that the sickness of the employment zone is the inevitable result of the shortcomings of human nature, and to demonstrate that it is, in fact, the reaction to conditions which we have as a nation the power to change.*

Not a political issue

There is something deeper than political differences at stake. The changes which are necessary – namely industrial justice for the individual, participation in the formation of the policies which managers operate, equitable payment, and full opportunity of employment – are changes which I believe are desired by all of us, whatever our political opinion may be.

These things can be achieved – not by trying to persuade people to behave differently but by recognizing that part of our National strategy and many of our industrial arrangements are relics of the past. We are weighed down by assumptions and conventions which are no longer relevant to the present. Industrial strife is caused not so much by human failings as by the social, economic, and constitutional environment in which we work. So to improve industrial relations we should first examine the assumptions on which we base our organization of industrial affairs. If any of these assumptions prove to be outdated we must drop them, thus enabling us to modify the relevant institutions and improve the working environment.

We must become more sceptical, more analytical, and more constructive. We must look at current procedures and decide whether or not they are sensible. If they are not, then each of us must bend our minds to the task of trying to work out better arrangements and summon the resolution to try and convince others that they are worth while. The least constructive attitude is to criticize existing conditions and reject proposals for improving them simply on the grounds that new ideas represent too great a change or seem too difficult to put into practice.

A failure to adapt to changing conditions

Failure to appreciate the need for adaptation of industrial institutions has forced people to break the bounds of the old institutions but new ones have not emerged to guide behaviour and contain conflict. This lack of innovation produces increasingly chaotic conditions in our docks, motor industry, printing industry, and elsewhere. Conflict and confusion is now beginning to appear in the public and social services.

I suggest that few of us, whatever our role in employment, are satisfied with the current state of affairs. It ought to be an exciting co-operative endeavour but often it does not seem at all like that. Most of us want to alter the situation but have great difficulty in formulating the changes which we want. These frustrated aspirations emerge in the form of criticism of others. The villains of the piece are variously picked out as being the directors, the managers, the workers, the shop stewards, the Trade Unions, or 'subversive elements'. But it is outmoded institutions which are at the root of our troubles, not groups of individuals.

Nevertheless, I detect a consistent theme running through this flow of recrimination. It is the cry for more communication, more participation, or more industrial democracy. Yet few of us want, for example, to see all managers elected, or all decisions taken by committees, or all industries to be owned by the state, or equality of earnings for all or some modern form of syndicalism. Most people accept that employment hierarchies, with their differentiated levels of pay, authority, and accountability, are essential if we are to maintain and improve the economic standards which we all desire. But we want these hierarchies to be more consistent with the democratic culture which pervades our lives as citizens.

What is to be done?

There is a school of thought which argues that all that is needed are the right incentives and that these will bring about the necessary widespread change in behaviour. Many Conservative politicians apparently believed that a reduction in income tax would inspire our people to make the employment zone more efficient. I have often heard people voice the view that people in industry choose not to work overtime because of income tax in spite of the fact that most managers' experience is that people insist on working overtime and often threaten strike action if it is reduced. There is another school of thought, largely stemming from the American business schools, which believes that people can be 'motivated', though the means suggested seem to me nothing less than an attempt to manipulate personality, and that is self-defeating.

I do not accept that the solution to the problems of the employment zone lies simply in 'more communication' or the 'stick and the carrot' or 'paternalism' or 'profit sharing' or 'Worker/Directors' or 'Job Evaluation' or 'Job Enrichment' or 'more nationalization' or in waiting for education to change attitudes. Nor do I believe in throwing in the sponge despairingly because the counter-productive attitudes which are emerging in employment are a function of existing industrial institutions. Given the will, these institutions can be changed relatively easily. I am convinced, on the basis of experience, that change in the behaviour of people will follow changes in the institutions.

I therefore propose that we set about the task of changing some of our economic and employment institutions. I do not believe that the changes needed are as drastic as they appear because, in a confused and muddled way, we have been moving towards those changes ever since 1945.

In the following chapters I shall first comment on the nature and the inevitability of employment hierarchies, and then describe the real nature of the managerial–subordinate relationship. I shall then discuss how we might achieve the four fundamental conditions required if we are to create an environment of work where people have a sense of fairness and creativity. These four conditions are: (*a*) clear employee right of appeal against felt injustice; (*b*) employee participation in policy making; (*c*) abundant employment; (*d*) equitable payment. But I shall deal with these matters not as political abstractions or as ideals to be aimed at but in terms of the specific institutions and organizational arrangements needed to make them inescapable and real.

My views stem from practical experience, application in an

industrial company, and constant reconsideration over a period of twenty-five years. Out of these have come perceptions of the changes which we must make in the environment within which the employment hierarchies operate, and of the changes which must take place in the way in which they are conducted in order to allow human creativity and satisfaction to express itself in efficient functioning at work. I believe that institutions which would provide abundant employment, equitable pay, participation in policy-making, the right of appeal, and access by all to full-scale managers, would go far to bring about the behaviour in all of us which we all want.

But it is useless to go on wishing the ends without wishing the means. We shall not get what we want without facing the need for institutional change. The root of the trouble is that few believe that institutional changes will produce the changed behaviour which society desperately needs. The effect on individual human behaviour of the shape taken by constitutions, laws, and organizational structures is not sufficiently understood or accepted. I hope that this book will do something towards making that connection.

CHAPTER 2

The inevitability of employment hierarchies

It is a commentary on the state of confusion in the employment zone that we have such a paucity of words for discussing its problems. When entrepreneurs or churches or armies or shareholders or football clubs or local authorities or governments want to employ people to get work done they set up pyramidal structures of roles with one man at the top accountable for all the work and descending layers of managers, specialists, supervisors, craftsmen, clerks, and operatives. There is no term in general use to refer to these pyramids of roles. It is as though nobody wanted to talk about them. I will refer to these pyramids, each containing strata of roles carrying differing levels of work, as employment hierarchies.

Employment hierarchies have existed through the ages but with some notable exceptions such as armed forces and the Church, they have in our earlier history usually employed small numbers. But today many industrial hierarchies are huge. A company which a hundred years ago employed a thousand people would have been regarded as large. Today it is regarded as small.

This rapid growth in size ought to have warned us. We ought to have devoted greater resources to the study of large employment hierarchies, for they are, in fact, social mechanisms of great complexity. But today, with ninety per cent of the working population spending a large part of their lives in roles within these hierarchies, little is known of the best means of structuring them. How does change of policy really come about? How many layers of managers are needed for a given amount and type of work? How many and what kinds of specialists are required? What should be the relationship between one type of role and another? How is the correct level of pay for different work to be decided? and so on. In a hierarchy employing a thousand people there are nine hundred and ninety-nine managerial–subordinate relations, and yet there is still no generally accepted definition of the term,

Manager. I have written elsewhere* about these problems of structure and relationship and will not pursue the subjects in detail here, but I want to get the idea of the employment hierarchy into focus as an all-pervading socio-economic institution upon which society is completely dependent and about which there exists much ignorance.

Employment hierarchies essential

Employment hierarchies have proved, over the last hundred years, to be much the most effective way of bringing the work of large numbers to bear on some common endeavour.

There have been thousands of attempts to find alternative forms of organization in many countries but, as far as I know, all have eventually been discarded because the employment hierarchy gets the work done more effectively and is the basis of our current economic standards of life.

It seems important to sift this matter thoroughly because if work hierarchies are to be with us permanently it is important that we should be convinced that that is so. Otherwise we may go on hoping and planning for something different and this will detract from the effort to make hierarchies better able to serve social as well as economic ends. It isn't very practical to dream of 'workers' control' or to regard any situation where some have authority over others as improper if in fact that could be achieved only at the expense of an unacceptable reduction in living standards.

There seems to be little doubt that home background, education, and social stratum exercise a great deal of influence on the career progression which follows. Many people accordingly seem to believe that if these factors were made more equal then we should find much less difference in skill, work capacity, and intellectual ability than seems to exist at present. This is probably correct, but differences of wide degree can be seen to exist among those whose early environment has been very similar, and vast numbers of people who have had an under-privileged start in life

* See Bibliography on page 122.

13

later disclose ability far exceeding those who have been more fortunate.

If we consult our personal experience of working within hierarchical organizations I think we would certainly agree that personal ability varies very greatly from person to person; and if indeed there are substantial genetically-based differences in the ability of people then the hierarchy is a form of work organization which has the potentiality of making full use of widely varying personal abilities.

Differing capacity of people

During the last war millions of people were subjected to interviews and various types of test to rate their potential capability by psychologists of the various branches of the armed forces. These supported the principle that intellectual capacity was distributed among people in accordance with the diagram in Figure 1.*

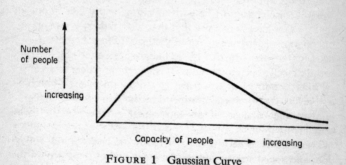

FIGURE 1   Gaussian Curve

Figure 2 uses exactly the same data about the capacity of people and their numbers but is drawn with the vertical scale of Figure 1 in the horizontal position and vice versa.

* Gauss, a German mathematician, put forward the theory that most human characteristics when plotted on a graph against the numbers in a population possessing those characteristics, produced a curve of the form I have shown in Figure 1. Such curves are called Gaussian Curves. A great deal of evidence has since accrued to suggest that his theory has validity.

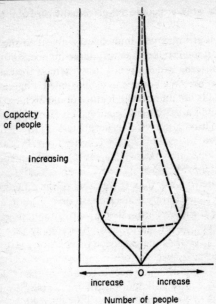

Capacity of people increasing

increase ← O → increase

Number of people

FIGURE 2   Amended Curve

I have inserted in a dotted line in Figure 2 a simplified indication of the general shape of an employment hierarchy.

These diagrams suggest that the distribution of capacity among large populations is similar to the distribution of talent required by employment hierarchies, although, of course, individual hierarchies may want disproportionate numbers of people of a certain grade. Perhaps it would be more accurate to say generally that hierarchies are a type of employment organization which can employ people of differing degrees of ability (with some similarity to the proportions in which those abilities occur) on work which matches those differing abilities. I do not suggest that this factor of general ability is the whole story. Suitability of training and temperament are important also. But it remains true that the organization of complex work requires an ascending degree of inherent intellectual ability to match the increasing

15

complexity of work as people travel from the base of the hierarchy to its apex.

I suspect that many will immediately object to the foregoing statements on the ground that very large numbers of people are employed on tasks which do not fully exercise their ability and that they are therefore bored and disillusioned. I agree the objection, but that is not an *essential* feature of hierarchies. This misfit of people to jobs arises largely because there is insufficient freedom for people to leave a job which is unsatisfactory to them and enter another where the level of work is a better fit to their ability. The existence of unemployment is the cause of this absence of freedom. Full employment, in my view, is an essential condition if hierarchies are to work well. If we think of the different levels of work to be carried out by a hierarchical organization as A, B, C, etc., A being the lowest level, then absurd situations can develop in the presence of unemployment. A company sets up a new factory and advertises the existence of vacancies. Most of them are jobs at level A. Because of unemployment the large number of applicants contains many people capable of B or C level work. Selection procedures will appoint the most able people and the final result is to have many A level jobs filled by people whose ability is much higher than that required. The mistake is then made of explaining the boredom and frustration which emerges by pointing to the 'soul-destroying monotony' of the type of work which modern industry produces. But the real cause of the trouble is not in the work but in a misfit between the ability of the person and the level of work in the role which he occupies, caused by the existence of unemployment and inadequate appointment procedures. I shall discuss means of overcoming unemployment in a later chapter.

A misfit of people to work can take place without the presence of unemployment when differential wages go adrift. If car assembly-line workers are paid more than teachers then some potential teachers might be lured by the higher pay into jobs which are well below their ability and boredom would result.

Many people will suggest that the growth of mechanization, automation, and computerization means not only an increase in unemployment but also a steady increase in the proportion of jobs which call for a low level of ability. Society is full of people who keep on insisting that more and more employees will be forced into low-level button-pushing jobs in the future. Happily, they are wrong. When a process is mechanized it may reduce machine-operator jobs from, say, twenty to ten, but it will usually create, say, three additional higher-level jobs in designing, tool making, and controlling. Thus, the *proportion* of low-level jobs is decreased. In my example mechanization has decreased the *total* of jobs by seven but that is the way to a higher standard of living for they are released to produce extra goods – *if there is employment for them*. That takes us again to the problem of unemployment, to be dealt with later.

I agree that the initial impact of the application of modern technology may seem to create many low-level jobs but in the long term the result is the opposite. Consider the situation on the farms, in the mines, and in the textile factories, during the early years of the industrial revolution. Millions were employed at that time, not to use their skill but as a form of physical energy. We have largely replaced human physical work with steam, oil, and electrical power. But consider the appalling boredom for a farm worker of unrecognized intelligence put to harvesting turnips by hand from a ten-acre field. Those indeed were the days of bore-dom, frustration, and physical exhaustion too. Modern technology doesn't increase the number of low-level jobs – it decreases it and increases the number of higher-level jobs.

The pessimists might consider why, if they are correct, it is today necessary to spend ever-increasing amounts on education for work. They might also take into account the fact that even in areas of the country where there are high rates of unemployment there is often a shortage of skilled people.

The ability of people changes

Despairing thoughts about the future of the employment zone arise also because of our relative ignorance of the nature of human ability. For example I wonder how many people realize that the level of ability of adults rises as they grow older. This rise in ability continues much longer than is generally assumed. In

Figure 3 below is a series of curves. These show the relationship between ability and age. They have been used internationally by a very large number of employers for many years and I have myself no doubt of their validity as a general comment on the changing ability of populations.*

Some are fortunate to have the sort of ability which follows the steeper curves. Others follow more modest rates of varying ability.

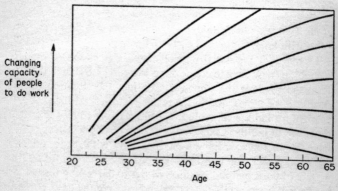

FIGURE 3   Progression Curves

However, many managers and employers continue to believe that ability in adults is a fixed quantity and that people 'reach their ceilings' at quite early ages. There is ample evidence to show that this is not so. The result of these unfounded assumptions is that people are denied opportunity for advance to higher levels of work despite the fact that their ability has grown, and will for

* Figure 3 is part of a larger graph which extends the top curves through to later ages. Critics have pointed out that these top curves imply that the maximum capacity of some people will not be reached until very late in life indeed. This is so, but it must be remembered that in most cases *physical* deterioration will set in before the development of maximum capacity. There are, however, numerous examples through history (and recent history) of great men showing immense ability at very advanced ages.

In order to shorten the text I have grossly over-simplified the origin of these curves. Chapter 9 of my book *Organization* (Heinemann Educational Books), or *Equitable Payment*, by Elliott Jaques (Heinemann Educational Books) both discuss these curves fully.

many years continue to grow. This is another source of the assertion that industry is creating more and more boring jobs.

Men whose ability is greater than is called for by their job have to leave one employer and seek a higher level of work with another company. But this is difficult to achieve because they cannot cite experience on that higher level of work. In any case it is a risky procedure if there is unemployment.

The need for knowledge

Faced with the task of building, repairing, or redesigning a complex machine, we will not, if we are wise, essay the task unless we first have a reasonable understanding of the function of each of its parts and the relation of one part to another. If we start without this knowledge we shall certainly have to acquire it as we proceed with the task. If we do not understand we come a cropper. Large employment hierarchies are vast social mechanisms which are much more important to human happiness than physical mechanisms. But we know much less about these social systems than we do about complex physical systems. The sad fact is that much of this knowledge is absent from the minds of those in charge of employment hierarchies. That is another reason why employment can often be an unsatisfactory experience for the individual.

These, then, are some of the reasons for quite widespread pessimism about employment hierarchies and about human nature. But I am an optimist because I believe that hierarchies can be designed to provide work roles which feel satisfying and creative to those who occupy them. We have much leeway to make up because these matters should have received due attention along with society's eager attention to technology and economics from the start of the Industrial Revolution. But it is not too late.

CHAPTER 3

The Manager–subordinate relationship

As I have already pointed out, if a company employs one thousand people, then it contains nine hundred and ninety-nine managerial–subordinate relationships, because every person employed has a manager except the chief executive. There are more of these relationships in employment hierarchies than any other type of formal relationship. They are of vital importance and yet no generally accepted definition of the term, Manager, exists.

The kind of manager for whom we work is a very important factor in deciding whether or not our work satisfies us. If we ourselves are managers, then our satisfaction also depends on our relationships with our subordinates.

Managerial behaviour depends on role clarity

Most people want to work for a manager who is honest, fair to others, experienced in work, efficient in practice, and friendly in discussion, and who has the guts to be decisive when facing problems. Few people seem to realize that a manager may possess such qualities and yet appear to lack them because his own authority and accountability have never been made clear. If a manager is not certain where he stands then he cannot place his own subordinates in a clear-cut position. The result is trouble in terms of human satisfaction and efficiency. Some people have a flair for carrying managerial roles, others have not, but even those who are well endowed cannot make a real success of managerial work if they remain uncertain about their authority and accountability. On the other hand, some people holding managerial roles are seriously deficient in appropriate ability but because of obscurity and uncertainty their deficiencies are not exposed and they remain in posts which they are ill-fitted to hold, to the grave detriment of their subordinates.

The essential point is that the behaviour of a manager results not only from his personal ability and character but also from the degree of clarity with which he is able to perceive the extent of his own accountability and authority.

Defining the term, Manager

I cannot discuss these very important relationships any further without defining what I mean by the term, Manager. None of us would have much difficulty in defining what we mean, say, by the term Borough Councillor as 'a person who is elected to the Council of a Borough, without opposition or by the majority vote of the electors in a ward, and who is accountable to all his constituents for the manner in which he represents their interests in taking part in the control of the affairs of the Borough'. But in defining we would not be describing the work of such a role. We should be drawing attention to the singular characteristics of such a role which distinguish it from other roles. My definition of manager will do no more than that.

A chief executive in charge of an employment hierarchy is accountable for the whole of the work done by everybody employed within it. His subordinates are accountable for those parts of the total work which the chief executive delegates to them and so on down through the descending ranks of managerial–subordinate layers to the base of the hierarchy. This means that there are many roles in the employment hierarchy where the work allotted to a single role is greater than the occupant of that role can personally perform. In order to get all the work of his role carried out the occupant of that role has to get some of it carried out by others. But, in spite of the fact that he does not do all the work in his role personally, he nevertheless is held responsible for all of it by higher authority. I believe those to be uncontestable statements of fact. Anybody familiar with employment situations can test these statements merely by thinking about them and comparing them with his experience.

Once those statements are accepted, then certain other statements follow if we are prepared to be strictly logical. Figure 4 is a diagram of a very simple employment hierarchy.

Consider the situation of B. He is given more work to do than he can *personally* perform. Therefore, he must delegate some of it

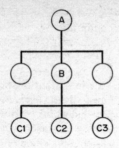

FIGURE 4   Managerial Hierarchy

to C1, C2, and C3. But he is held accountable by A for all the work in his role. If B is to be accountable in this way, then certain conditions are inevitable.

A manager's right to veto the appointments of subordinates

B must be able to veto the appointment of people to roles C1, C2, and C3. For if A says 'I am going to appoint Joe to role C1' and B says 'Joe has not got the skill or knowledge to do the work which I shall have to allot to him and he will fail me', then, if A insists, A cannot hold B accountable for that portion of his work which is done for him by C1. *Therefore a manager must be able to veto appointments to roles immediately subordinate to him.*

The authority of B to veto appointments does not give him the right to have anyone of his choice as a subordinate. That is why I use the word 'veto' rather than say that B has the right to make 'appointments' to immediately subordinate roles. In other words, B cannot appoint his 'blue-eyed boys' unless A also agrees.

A second reason for not giving B the full choice of subordinates is because those subordinates should, as they gain experience and increase in ability, be candidates for positions immediately subordinate to A. So A is deeply concerned with those appointments, though not in the immediate present.

An analysis of the situation in most employment hierarchies would show that the situation I have described about appointments is not uncommon. But few managers will, on being questioned, immediately describe the situation in my way. If, however, you put my words to them, they will, after thought, agree. The arrangement is not explicitly understood and because it is not fully comprehended it will not be adhered to consistently. That is where trouble arises.

In some hierarchies it will be found that B has simply to accept, as subordinates, people who are selected by a personnel department without right of questioning their choices. In such a case B is clearly not in managerial command of C1, C2, and C3.

The character of managers gets distorted in the eyes of their subordinates when they lack this essential authority. Take the example of a General Manager, a Works Manager, his subordinate, a Foreman in charge of Section X, and 'Joe', a very experienced craftsman. The foreman retires from the job. The employees in Section X all expect 'Joe' to be appointed in his place. When a person from outside the company gets the job everybody feels that the Works Manager has acted unfairly. This blemishes his reputation. But the Works Manager has no explicit right of veto against the appointment of persons as his subordinates. The General Manager refused to appoint 'Joe' (though he had no personal knowledge of his qualities) because he thought that 'new blood was needed', etc., etc. The Works Manager had wanted Joe and argued the case for his promotion but was overruled. If the Works Manager had had the authority which managers really need, he would have been able to veto the General Manager's choice and might have got 'Joe' instead. The employees blamed the Works Manager unjustly, because they didn't know where authority resided.

A manager's authority to assess the work of subordinates

B must also be able to decide how to split up his work between C1, C2, and C3, based on his assessments of their relative ability. This is also logical because if A says 'give that part of your work to C2' and B says 'C2 cannot do it as well as C3' but A insists, then he cannot hold B accountable for the poor way in which that part of B's work is done for him by C2. *So B logically must have the right to decide who is most or least capable among his subordinates*

23

and the right to allocate work to them in the way in which he decides.

The right to be the sole judge of the different abilities of immediate subordinates is very important. Many people will have strong objections to the endowing of managers with this right. They will argue that this gives the manager too much power and that it can lead to undignified conduct on the part of a subordinate to curry favour with his manager. But the fact is that nobody else can make these differential assessments of the work of a manager's subordinates. The manager once removed is judging the manager of those subordinates. To revert to Figure 4, A is assessing B on the basis of B's work and the contribution to that work made by C1 and C2. A does not know what portion of B's work B has allocated to C1 and C2. The real danger lies in the possibility of A trying to make differential assessments of subordinates who are at one remove from him. Such assessments would necessarily be based on very superficial factors. If in fact B is a bad manager and is behaving unjustly, then it is difficult to hide, especially if appeal procedures exist, representatives are alert and A is watching the behaviour of B as he should be doing.

If a manager is not given authority to make these differential assessments of his immediate subordinates, then he will lose the respect of those subordinates.

For example a complex new machine tool is installed. 'Joe' has always been regarded as the most highly skilled man in the section. Everybody expects him to be asked by their Foreman to take charge of the new machine. When 'Harry' is given the job everybody feels that it is grossly unfair. But they don't know that the Works Manager over-rode the Foreman's decision. So the Foreman is regarded as an unfair person.

A manager's authority to 'de-select' subordinates

Lastly, if, say, C1 has demonstrated to B over a reasonable period that he is not capable of carrying out the work delegated to him to a standard which meets with B's approval, then B must have the right to insist that he is removed and replaced by someone else. If A insists that C1 remains in his role when it has been reasonably established that his work does not meet the required standard, then, logically speaking, A cannot hold B accountable for that portion of B's work which he will be forced to continue to allot to C1.

This does not mean that B can discharge C1 from the employment hierarchy. *B must logically have the limited right of ejecting the occupant of C1's post from that role – with the possibility that he could be transferred to some other role.* There is no word in common usage to describe this limited right of B because the words 'dismiss, discharge, fire, sack', etc., mean to most people removal from the whole employment hierarchy. I, therefore, would like to see the term 'de-select' come into use because the right of B really is to reverse the original process of selecting someone for the post to which C1 was appointed. (It would be unsatisfactory to use the alternative term 'disappoint'.)

Lack of authority to de-select can have a serious effect on a manager's relationships with his immediate subordinates. For example, manager B is very dependent upon the capabilities and performance of his subordinates. If they fail to perform adequately, then manager B fails to get *his* work done properly. Manager B will be assessed by manager A and may lose his own job. But if, say, C1 wins money in a football pool and decides he is going to enjoy it by constantly taking days off work and continues to do so in spite of B's warnings, then what does B do if he hasn't the authority to remove C1?

Suppose 'Joe' has been consistently late in turning up for work for months. Every time this happens, others have to fill in for him until he arrives. The whole section is fed up and so is the Foreman. He starts to tackle the problem with a series of warnings to 'Joe' but without improvement. Finally the Foreman decides that 'Joe' must leave the section and before informing 'Joe' he tells the Plant Manager. The Plant Manager says, 'No – you can't do that – we might have a strike on our hands.' The Foreman argues but to no avail, so 'Joe' stays. The effect is that every member of the section feels 'Well, if Joe can get away with it, then we needn't bother about time-keeping.' All take the Foreman's *apparent* tolerance as a sign of relaxation of a necessary code of conduct.

I have given a boundary definition of the role of a 'manager' by pointing out the unique characteristics of the manager–subordinate relationship in terms of accountability and authority. In doing so let it be clear that I have not described the work of a manager. We cannot define institutions by describing the way in which they are used. Definitions of social institutions have to be worded in such a way that a reasonable person can decide whether the institution which he observes does or does not fall within the ambit of the definition.

Using this definition of manager it is possible by asking three questions to define whether or not a person is in a managerial role: can you veto appointments? are you solely responsible for making *differential* assessments of subordinates? can you de-select subordinates?

If the answer to all these questions is 'yes', then the role is a managerial one.

It is very important to be able to discover the answer to these questions. Many employees are separated from their manager by an intermediary who, though apparently their manager, has not got managerial accountability and authority. Such persons then find themselves in this position: their straw-boss (to use an American term) *knows* their capability but *cannot* make consequential decisions: their manager *does not know* their capability and *does* make decisions which affect them. This situation could and should be cleared up in every employment hierarchy.

In many of the workshops of British industry there is real confusion. We find 'leading hands', 'charge hands', 'assistant foremen', 'foremen', and 'supervisors'. Few of them know the bounds of their accountability and authority. As no definition of the term manager is in current use, nobody knows whether or not they are managers. There is delay and uncertainty about the making of decisions and when these decisions affect conditions of work, pay, and other matters of importance to the individual, then trouble is generated. This is certainly one of the areas of confusion which must be cleared up if the employment zone is to be improved.

Reasons for failure to delegate managerial authority

I suspect that delegation isn't made for the following reasons:

(1) Hierarchies without arrangements which give every employee the right of individual appeal to higher levels of authority dare not delegate the authority required. People in command of such hierarchies are afraid that if straw-bosses are given real managerial authority they might wield it unfairly. Then, in the absence of the right of appeal, they might have trouble or strikes on their hands.
(2) The authority of managers has to be limited to an area bounded by policies. Many hierarchies have few explicit policies. Thus if they give authority to straw-bosses they feel that they are giving almost unlimited authority. This they cannot do.
(3) Policies exist about working conditions in many hierarchies which have never been agreed by representatives. Senior managers can't delegate managerial authority to implement such policies because they are quite uncertain as to what would happen if they did. In the absence of established means of getting their policies about working conditions agreed by representatives, they are stuck with the position. They are frozen into inaction.

I have had the experience of establishing appeal mechanisms and formal means of agreeing policies about working conditions and then establishing real managerial roles. It is not easy to do this. Many foremen, office managers, etc., when given managerial authority in real terms proved unwilling to use it or incapable of using it. The transformation to a situation where everybody was directly accountable to a real manager and had right of access to him took time to bring about. But the long-term effect was a real improvement in morale, discipline, and output, and much better manager–subordinate relationships.

I believe that employment hierarchies are inevitable but much more insight into their working is required by all employed within them. Employment hierarchies are built around a series of ascending manager–subordinate relationships and both subordinates and managers have the right to know the precise form of this relationship in terms of tasks, accountability, authority, and the policies which circumscribe that authority. But these matters are not clear. Not until they have been clarified will we have done all that can be done to better the situation in the employment zone.

CHAPTER 4

Right of appeal for individual employees

It took centuries to establish the right of the citizen to appeal to the courts against the actions of civic and government authorities. Today this right is regarded as one of the pillars of freedom. Any government proposal which even *seems* to hold the possibility of reducing this right arouses strong opposition in Parliament and protest elsewhere. It is therefore extraordinary that for so long no such right of appeal by employees against the decisions of managers has been considered to be necessary.

I find it difficult to argue the case for appeal mechanisms which are freely open to all employees because the supporting reasons seem almost too obvious to state.

Managers are an essential feature of employment hierarchies. Managers make decisions which have very important results for their subordinates, but they are human and they make mistakes. Therefore individuals who feel that mistaken decisions have been taken must be able to raise such issues with somebody other than the manager who made the decisions in order that they can be reviewed. Clearly such right of appeal is one of the essential freedoms if the employment zone is to be organized in a manner which takes account of human feeling and dignity.

As a chief executive of a large company I caused an appeal procedure to be set up in 1941. There was initial apprehension from many managers and foremen but within months these had disappeared. Now, thirty years later, if a manager of that company were to be asked why the company continues to operate such a procedure I think his response would be to regard the questioner as eccentric.

In principle, any employee ought to have the right to say to his manager either 'I think you have exceeded your authority in taking that decision and I appeal' or 'that decision is unfair to me and I wish to appeal'. I want every employee to have his appeal heard by his manager's manager. I want the employee, if he loses his first appeal, to be able to go on appealing until he reaches the chief executive or, in the case of large companies with establishments in many parts of the country, to the chief executive in the area. Some may believe that this unlimited right of appeal will result in the raising of a multitude of frivolous grievances. Such is not my experience. The details of an appeal system (which appear in the Appendix) suggest that appellants must also have the right to the assistance of a representative in pursuing their appeals. Representatives, again in my experience, are always called upon to assist an appellant in this way. It is the representative, so approached, who customarily eliminates the really frivolous appeals. The real problem is not too many frivolous appeals, but, rather, a failure of employees to appeal when they should have done so.

I have been actively advocating the adoption of appeal procedures in industry for twenty years. I have occasionally met others with the same view. Few people produce arguments against such ideas and yet so many companies shrink from them. Trade Union power could get them rapidly introduced but I have yet to hear of a strike organized to insist on the right of appeal for the individual.

Clearly therefore this essential freedom cannot be won by a simple statement of the obvious arguments. There are deep resistances at work. I shall explore these. The benefits are not clear. I shall state them. Confusion exists as to the form which appeal procedures should take. I shall describe a system which has worked successfully for many years. Anxiety exists about the behaviour which appeals systems might generate. I shall describe the results of the system which I initiated.

Some recent progress

But before moving into these issues let us take stock of the current situation because there has been some recent progress.

The Industrial Relations Act, 1971, has for the first time in British law given employees a clear right of appeal against managerial decisions, but it deals only with a tiny percentage of the felt injustices which arise. It provides right of appeal to an external tribunal for an employee who feels that he has been unfairly dismissed, but only if he has already been employed by the company for a minimum of two years. That does not take us very far because most potential appeals are about other matters. It is also unfortunate that those who drafted the Act failed fully to realize the substantial differences between civil appeals to the courts and industrial appeals. The result has been the emphasis on appeals to external tribunals. Clearly as soon as this had been decided upon as an important principle it became necessary to limit the subject of appeal to that of dismissal. If the Act had allowed appeals about other matters to external tribunals, then the tribunals might have been swamped with work. In addition, if an external body is to be used, then it will require extensive briefing on all the circumstances. The prospect for managers of having to keep records of every complaint in case it went to appeal would be very daunting indeed.

The Act should have provided for internal appeals conducted in accordance with the procedures which I have set out in the Appendix to this book. The Act could then safely have specified the right of every employee to insist that *any* decision by his manager should be reviewed by successively higher stages of managerial authority.

In fact, Section 31 of the Act does cover the establishment of procedural agreements between management and trade unions which could cover the subject of internal appeals, and Section 31 (2) (e), though obscurely worded, does make it possible to introduce into such a procedural agreement provisions which may have the result that few appeals will have to be heard by an external tribunal. On the whole, however, the Act is deficient on the subject of industrial appeals and it may inhibit progress.

The Industrial Relations Code,* which is separate from the Act, has a good deal to say about 'grievance' procedures.

---

* In its own words, 'The Code imposes no legal obligations. Failure to observe it does not by itself render anyone liable to proceedings. But Section 4 of the Industrial Relations Act requires any relevant provisions to be taken into account in proceedings under the Act before the National Industrial Relations Court or an Industrial Tribunal.' In other words, if you break the code you will prejudice your case before the courts in any hearing about a dispute.

Paragraph 16 says that employers' associations should encourage their members to develop arrangements for settling grievances.

Paragraph 60 says that every employee is entitled to be notified in writing of how he can seek redress for a grievance.

Paragraph 91 says that procedures should include means of settling individual grievances.

Paragraph 121 says that Management and Representatives should jointly establish formal procedures under which individual employees can raise grievances and have them settled promptly and fairly.

Paragraph 123 perpetuates a real howler about grievances which I shall state and criticize later.

Those are the main references in the code and it is certainly good to see them there, but what a pity that the code could not have been clearer and gone further. In the first place why refer to them consistently as 'grievance procedures'? People in industry will say such things as, 'the boss has a grievance against me' or 'Joe has a grievance against the foreman'. The word often carries the sense of an *unjustified* complaint. Many companies will claim that they already have a grievance procedure but it certainly is not what I mean by an appeal procedure; as I shall show.

The word 'appeal' doesn't appear in the code. It means 'call *to* (higher tribunal) for deliverance from decision of lower'.* This dictionary meaning carries the right flavour in the sense that it is easily interpreted as 'call upon a higher manager to reverse the judgement of a lower one'.

In order to protect the shareholders, the Companies Act, 1948, insists that a company must deposit with the Registrar of Companies, for approval, a copy of the regulations it proposes to use for managing its financial affairs. If it does not do so it will have to adopt the model regulations set out in an appendix to the Act. What an excellent precedent this is for adoption by the Industrial Relations Code. It was a pity that a model appeal system did not appear in an appendix to the code to be used in the same way. Reading the 1948 and 1967 Companies Acts makes one realize how much more Parliament has been exercised to safeguard the

* *Concise Oxford English Dictionary.*

rights of shareholders than to safeguard the rights of employees. The difference in treatment is astounding and makes one realize why organized labour, being denied the constitutional means of defending the individual, has instead resorted so often to the use of its power to strike. But despite these criticisms the code is a definite advance on what existed before.

Resistances to appeal procedures

There are still in existence some managers who consider themselves benefactors because they are 'providing employment' for people who ought therefore obediently to accept whatever decisions they choose to make. But a person who takes initiatives which lead to the employment of others is in no way released from the moral duty of organizing that employment wisely, humanely, and efficiently. Appeal procedures should be part of any sound organization.

There are other managers who think in terms of 'managerial prerogatives' which they interpret as a natural right to enforce some types of decisions, usually unspecified, however objectionable they may be to other employees. Appeal procedures are anathema to such managers.

Thank goodness both of these types of managers are a dying race. Their forebears bear much of the responsibility for our current industrial relations problems.

Managerial fears of the results of the right of appeal

Managers commonly have illusory fears of what will happen if an appeal system is introduced; for example, 'Every third decision of every manager will be challenged – we shall spend so much time hearing appeals that we won't be able to get on with the job . . .' In my experience there were many appeals – as a chief executive I used to hear an average of ten to twelve each year. There were many more at lower levels which were settled before they reached me. But there was a very large net saving of time because of the reduction of argument and negotiation over the same issues with representatives.

Another illusion is the idea that 'only our foremen really understand the chaps and their feelings – if right of appeal is allowed to higher managers they will never understand what is going on on the shop floor – leave it to the foremen and back their judgement through thick and thin'. But factory managers can decide whether agreed policies have been broken or not and they are perfectly capable of recognizing injustice where it exists.

Managers who take a poor view of human nature always resist extensions of human rights and their pessimism about people is reinforced by the protest which follows such denial. The Victorians were authoritarians and were prepared to concede reform only under great pressure. But despite widespread views to the contrary we are a much less vicious and violent society today than in their time.

Many managers fear that appeal systems will undermine their status and reduce their authority below the minimum necessary to enable them to operate a company successfully. I can understand their anxiety, but it is unjustified because in my experience the converse is true. The law courts do not undermine police authority. The reverse is the case. If there were no appeal against arbitrary acts of the police, then their authority would fall into contempt and anarchy would begin to encroach on civic authority.

The absence of institutionalized right of appeal causes employees to feel, rightly or wrongly, that managerial decisions are arbitrary. This is the psychological feeling which in turn convinces employees of the need to maintain solidarity and use threats of strike action to force review or reversal of managerial decisions. Thus the apparent paradox that the opening up of channels through which managerial decisions can be reviewed, and if necessary reversed, actually in my experience enhances the authority of managers.

I intend to discuss employee participation in policy-making in the next chapter. This participation is capable of producing a range of agreed policies covering wage structure, working hours, appointments, promotion, assessment of individuals, absence, redundancy, night shifts, overtime, and so on. It is the existence of such policies which puts boundaries round the area over which managers exercise authority and *which gives real authority to managers when they keep within these bounds*. But if bounds to authority are set up by agreement, then there must be means of adjudicating whether or not managers have gone outside such bounds.

In my experience most appeals were to the effect that the bounds had been exceeded. Some appeals were to the effect that though the bounds had not been exceeded the manager's decision was nevertheless unfair to his subordinate. I found that because a range of agreed policies and an appeal system both existed, the whole atmosphere of employment was much more relaxed. The result was that our appeals, instead of being angry disputes, had something of the more objective character of a court of law. Sometimes a manager's decisions were reversed but there was no sense of triumph on the part of the successful appellant. More often than not appellants lost their appeals because the existence of the appeal system had the effect of causing managers to give much more thought before making decisions. In addition the existence of an agreed range of policies made it much easier for managers to make decisions which were consistent and which clearly lay within the bounds of their authority.

Prior to the existence of formal right of appeal I was sometimes approached by employees (who were not my immediate subordinates) with the opening gambit 'Can I have a word with you?' My heart used to sink because often I was about to hear a complaint. I used to say, 'Have you seen your foreman?' The answer was usually, 'Yes, it's his decision I dispute.' What is a higher manager to do in such circumstances? When the appeal system was introduced the answer was easy. 'Have you appealed?' When the answer was often 'No', I used to say, 'If your complaint is not sufficiently important to you to cause you to take the trouble to appeal then I don't think you should trouble me. If you do appeal and don't get a decision which satisfies you at lower levels I shall eventually hear your appeal.' That was, I think, a reasonable answer. Shop stewards told me that they were often able to deal with complaints made to them in a similar way. They used to say, 'I'll help you lodge and conduct an appeal but if that is too much trouble you had better forget what's biting you because it can't be very important.'

In short, an appeal system does not introduce an era of loss of authority and lawlessness as some managers fear. The result is the reverse of this.

Do Trade Unions resist the introduction of appeal procedures?

Clearly many Trade Union officials and Shop Stewards are worried about the introduction of appeal procedures because if they had wanted them they could easily have negotiated them into existence. It is not so easy for me to describe the sources of their resistance. I can only make some guesses:

Paragraph 123 of the Industrial Relations Code of Practice says this – 'Individual and collective disputes are often dealt with by the same procedures. Where there are separate procedures they should be linked so that an issue can, if necessary, pass from one to the other, since a grievance may develop into a dispute.'

This is the howler I referred to earlier. It is indeed all too true that 'individual grievances and collective disputes are often dealt with through the same procedures'. That is a source of great trouble. To suggest that where they are separate they should be linked together is wrong. If a group of employees have a shared grievance it is usually in fact a challenge to some policy and is therefore a matter for negotiation. If the grievance is limited to an individual it can usually be settled quite quickly by an appeal procedure as long as a lot of other people are not sucked into the issue – which is exactly what happens if the same procedures are used both for grievances and for disputes about policies.

I believe that Trade Unions believe that the establishment of individual appeal procedures will weaken or disrupt their negotiating procedures. I do not think their anxieties are well-founded. In my own experience neither the five unions concerned nor their shop stewards ever raised this point after their own experience of the operations of our appeal procedure.

Judges in our courts of law have no axes to grind. Perhaps Trade Unions feel that, in contrast, the successively higher managers who would hear appeals under the system which I advocate are in a biased position and cannot therefore make just decisions. It is clear that there are many pressures on managers hearing appeals to support the decisions of their subordinate managers, in order perhaps to keep costs down or to hide injustice or to rid themselves of people who raise too many awkward questions. But on the other hand managers are well aware that if injustice is not rectified, then the loss of production which might arise from the trouble which followed would certainly not justify any silly attempt to thwart the course of justice. I have put this matter into quite a cynical perspective in order to bring into focus the arguments which probably weigh with Trade Unions. Thus, balancing pressure is always present because of the readiness of representatives and their Unions to use their great power to take disruptive action if the final managerial decision is, in their opinion, unjust.

Are these the reasons for Trade Union lack of interest in individual appeal procedure? Did they suggest to the Department of Employment the linking together of individual appeals and disputes procedures? In my view they should be kept quite separate so that individual complaints can be dealt with calmly and logically as such. Only when it is felt that injustice remains after the chief executive has heard the appeal should the issue become one of negotiation with representatives. Opportunity for such final negotiation was part of the procedure which operated when I was chief executive. But I cannot remember an occasion when it had to be used.

Difference between civil and industrial appeals

Some may feel that to allow negotiation between management and representatives in the event of the chief executive's final decision about an appeal being felt to be unjust is not in accord with judicial principles. It certainly is not. It would wreck our judicial systems if the final judgements of the House of Lords became a matter of later negotiation between the parties concerned. But appeal systems in employment hierarchies are not analogous to our civil judicial processes. Industry has to deal with very large numbers of relatively minor instances of feelings of injustice of a kind which do not arise in our civil and criminal courts. It was, I think, failure on the part of the Government to appreciate the difference which has rendered the Industrial Relations Act quite inadequate on the subject of appeal procedures.

The benefits of appeal procedures

An unhappy characteristic of the pattern of strikes in British industry is the high proportion of unofficial strikes. It is clear, even from a reading of the superficial accounts which appear in the press, that many of these arise out of incidents which originally affected one individual only. I am constantly left with the impression that had individual rights of appeal existed, the conflict would not have taken place, and I firmly believe that an appeal mechanism can prevent many such strikes. Perhaps more important, it creates a sense of fairness which eliminates the feelings of rancour often held by a proportion of employees in workshops or offices, which help to maintain a general relation of suspicion between employees and management in large establishments.

If a clear right of individual appeal does not exist, then an employee who is subject to what he feels is unfair treatment necessarily has to try to get his representative to raise the issue on his behalf. Perhaps in itself the issue is *relatively* trivial, though it never feels trivial to the employee affected. The shop steward is in difficulty because he cannot keep on raising small issues. So, beleaguered by his constituents over a period of time, he decides that 'there is too much of this sort of thing going on'. He decides to challenge 'management'. One issue is seized upon, generalized, understandably exaggerated, and the fight is on: 'management' investigates and, finding that the issue is indeed *relatively* trivial, concludes that the shop stewards have decided to become 'bloody-minded'. People in 'management' decide that they had better 'Take a stand'. They often fail to realize that this is the result of a series of small issues, of which one has been seized upon as a specific case of a more general failure on the part of some managers to make their decisions with due reference to existing policies and to the feelings of individuals.

Each of the previous irritating incidents could have been solved with a single appeal hearing at one higher level of management.

The manager hearing such appeals would have realized that one or more of his subordinate managers was behaving stupidly. Had he known he could have corrected that behaviour but he did not know because he lacked the feed-back of information which could have been provided by the right of appeal.

Managers, particularly those at the base of the hierarchy, are very busy people. They make mistakes and sometimes say stupid things, like everyone else, but without an appeal system there is no feed-back to higher managers and no mechanism for correction. So a series of little problems each capable of simple solution in its own right piles up and produces a major outburst. Managers have at last learnt that concentration on production, efficiency, budgets, and the like, to the exclusion of attention to human factors in fact *reduces* efficiency. But we have not yet sufficiently realized that it is necessary to institutionalize the methods by which due attention is paid to the human factor. One of these missing institutions is the right of appeal for individual employees.

A workable appeal procedure

This might have been the appropriate place to set out the details of an appeal system. But like the other institutions which I am discussing in this book it is really part of a package. Therefore I have described all these institutions in a general procedural agreement which appears in the Appendix.

The results of operating an appeal procedure

In the company upon which my experience is mainly based, from 1941 till 1965 there was one strike lasting one week in one of the company's plants. I cannot speak with the same certainty of the period since 1965 but I am not aware that any strikes have taken place since.*

* There were several 'strikes' lasting one or two days which were called nationally by the Confederation of Engineering Unions in support of one or other of their negotiations but these were not disputes with the company. Such involved union members in either breaking their contracts of employment or their obligations as members of a Trade Union – an awkward decision for every employee to take. It was agreed that the action any employee took was a matter of conscience.

Perhaps some might regard that as the major result of the appeal procedure. But I do not think so. The major results were fourfold. It forced management to get a whole range of policies explicitly agreed in writing with representatives in order that managers could clearly see the area over which they must exercise authority and discipline and equally to know the bounds to that authority. Managers thus came to know accurately which types of decision they could and must make and which lay outside the bounds of their authority.

For example, the decisions as to who should or should not work overtime had always previously been troublesome. The agreed policy which emerged was this. Every employee who was fit agreed on appointment to work up to thirty hours overtime per month on instruction from his manager *subject* to receiving thirty-six hours notice of the need. If he had already worked thirty hours or if thirty-six hours notice could not be given, then a manager could *request* him to work but not instruct him. I remember the case of a manager who, without being able to give thirty-six hours notice, made a request to a subordinate to work overtime. The employee said he could not because of family arrangements. The manager threatened that the employee would lose future overtime work if he did not comply. The employee appealed and won his case. The manager was severely reprimanded. I wonder how many foremen in industry use unfair pressure like that – and get away with it.

The procedure disclosed the existence of some managers with unsuitable personal characteristics and it caused others to think much more carefully before they acted.

The procedure created a general feeling of lawfulness which provided employees with a greater sense of security and managers with heightened authority to do what was right and necessary. This improved rather than detracted (as many fear) from the relationships between managers and subordinates.

It enhanced the rate of change and the degree of readiness to accept this. Changes are often feared by employees because they may have unforeseen effects. But if such effects are subject to appeal, then the fears are diminished.

In closing my comment on appeals I must again emphasize the

interdependence of the institutions I am describing in separate chapters. I can't visualize abundant employment without a new approach to achieving equitable differential rewards according to the level of work, or the maintenance of a system of equitable rewards without appeal procedures for individuals who feel un-justly treated. I can't visualize appeal procedures operating really successfully except in the presence of clearly defined manager–subordinate relations. I can't visualize people being prepared to accept the grant of the necessary authority to managers unless appeal procedures exist against misuse of this authority. I can't visualize managers using their authority justly and consistently unless explicit, uniform, policies limiting that authority exist. I can't visualize the acceptance of such policies by subordinates unless their representatives have participated in the formulation and, finally, I can't visualize that confident and reasonable frame of mind of representatives, which is required for participation in effective policy-making, if lack of creative opportunity and fear of unemployment hangs over them.

CHAPTER 5

The right of full participation by employee representatives in policy making

'More participation' has always been the cry of many who are subject to the authority of others. Today it is becoming a pressing demand. Participation goes under a variety of names – more consultation, more communication, election of employees to the board, industrial democracy, and so on, but there is an absence of clear formulation of the aspirations the words are intended to express.

Current confusion about participation

If a major portion of the population in a democratic society want something sufficiently, then, in the long run, they will probably achieve a measure of it at least. But failure to formulate the ideas and describe how they can be introduced without major disruption is causing anxious resistance to advance by those in authority. There is too much sloganizing and too little hard thinking about the whole issue of participation. Managers are alarmed by the topic because they are often convinced that it will take out of their hands the authority for making the decisions that are necessary to efficient operation, leaving them with accountability without authority. The more emotional spokesmen who lead the drive for participation talk about full industrial democracy without being able to specify what they mean. Their utterances enhance the anxiety of the managers.

I wonder how many members of the general public who do not work in our larger industries and services fully realize the difficulties which managers face in some of these. Managerial authority has been so seriously eroded by the power of representatives, supported, often reluctantly, by Trade Union officials, that reasonably efficient operation has become impossible. Power is not being used to promote the well-being of the enterprises but simply to deprive managers of authority. This use of power has not therefore provided employees with a sense of participation in running the enterprise. This sense of failure seems to exacerbate the desire to make still further use of power in a disruptive fashion. If we consider some (and only some) of our docks, shipyards, motorcar factories, airports, engineering factories, and printing establishments, we must be driven to the conclusion that new thinking has to be done.

I believe that it is possible by a careful analysis of how employment hierarchies actually function to propose arrangements which might match the aspirations of those who seek more participation and at the same time increase, in an entirely acceptable manner, the authority of managers.

The fears of managers about participation

There are advocates of 'more participation' who propose that *every* managerial decision be submitted to democratic consent of the employees; but the Trades Union Congress, earlier this century, rejected such notions. Society in general recognizes that employment hierarchies could not function in that manner if material progress is to be maintained. In spite of this many of the opponents of 'more participation' seem to fear that it will lead to a situation where managers will have to obtain consent of employees before every decision. This fantasy is reinforced by the failure of those who seek more participation to make clear what they mean when they use the word. In the resultant confusion two things happen. Managers, in fear of loss of all decision-making authority, from time to time take up stances in defence of 'managerial rights'. Very often these are ill-chosen and they thus find themselves in a position where they are insisting on their right to introduce changes which lie well outside any previously agreed policy. Employee representatives, facing what they believe to be the autocratic insistence of managers to make any decision which they choose, take up stances which at times are equally ill-chosen and commit their constituents to strike action against managerial decisions which lie well within the ambit of existing policies. The effect of such actions is to convince both sides to the argument that either management will win the struggle and make all the policies and the decisions, or employees will win and managers will largely be deprived of the ability to manage.

Employment hierarchies are not essentially autocratic

An employment hierarchy is a series of manager–subordinate relationships. It is normally described in terms like the following:

The chief executive is accountable for the total series of tasks for which the hierarchy has been established. He cannot be held accountable unless he possesses the right to make decisions concerning the strategy of the organization, the allocation of his work to subordinates, and the detailed manner in which that work is to be carried out. He must be able to make such decisions whether or not they meet with the approval of his subordinates because otherwise he could not be held accountable.

But the foregoing is an over-simplified description of the situation and it is that over-simplification which causes the tendency to regard employment hierarchies as autocratic by nature.

The chief executive cannot make any decision he chooses. First, he is limited by the law in many directions and, second, he is limited by policies set by higher bodies such as the Board of Directors in commercial companies. Next, he is limited by his customers with their power to refuse contracts if the price and quality of his products do not appeal and, lastly, he is limited by his own employees by their forceful insistence on satisfactory conditions of work and pay. All these limiting bodies have, in the last analysis, the power (legal or otherwise) to prevent a chief executive from implementing the decision which he may wish to take. The Board and shareholders through their power to dismiss the chief executive, the customers through their right to withdraw their custom, and the employees through their power to strike, can each close the company down.

The effect is that a chief executive is continually working within policies (often not explicitly stated) which are set by these three power groups. When a chief executive wishes to make important decisions which lie outside the ambit of previously agreed policies, then he must get new policies agreed by the power groups whose interests are affected by the changes which he wishes to make.

These are not opinions, they are facts. Yet they are constantly denied. Many commentators continue to assert that shareholders have no control over companies, and yet repeated occasions arise when they insist on drastic changes. No doubt shareholders often fail to exercise sufficient control but undoubtedly they possess the power to do so.

The suggestion that management possesses autocratic authority over employees is even more inaccurate because managers know that they can change nothing if opposed by a resolute body of representatives. Moreover, managers have the repeated experience of having to vary what they regard as appropriate policies in what they regard as an unsatisfactory way under threat of disruptive action by representatives.

The fundamental difference between the power of shareholders and that of employees is that the former have legal power whereas the latter have to resort to force. This difference points to what I believe is the real desire, however ill-expressed, of those who call for more participation. Employees want their representatives to be given constitutional authority to insist on maintenance of the *status quo* until changes proposed by management have been agreed or until amendments have been worked out which make the changes acceptable. Such constitutional authority would make it unnecessary for representatives to resort to the use of force. Grant of constitutional authority* in this form has, in my experience, substituted reasoned discussion, compromise, and amendment, for the use of threats of disruptive action.

The difference between policies and decisions

The most important element in all human work is the exercise of judgement, towards some objective, within bounds imposed by policies. We can think therefore of the prescribed element of work, (policies) and the discretionary element (decisions). Nobody can make any decisions they choose; everybody works

* The Netherlands Government 1971 Works Council Law has gone a long way to create such a situation. Every enterprise employing more than one hundred persons must set up a Works Council. Over some issues defined in the law the management may not make changes without the approval of the Works Council.

within a framework of policies even though many of these policies are not explicitly stated.

The constitutional authority to prevent change until it is agreed, which I suggest should be given to representatives of employees, would be authority over changes in policies – not authority over managerial decisions in implementation of those policies.

I believe that this analysis, in principle, resolves the argument over increased participation. If we can set up the appropriate institution within an employment hierarchy then the latter would find itself in the following situation. It would have to make its policies about working conditions explicit and to code them. No change could be made in them without the agreement of the representatives of all employees who might be affected. Once a policy was agreed, then management would have the full authority to make the decisions necessary to implement that policy. In experience over many years I found that once the necessary institution was created then participation was felt by employees to be real and the authority of managers was increased. Representatives questioned managerial decisions whenever they felt that these might be infringing agreed policy – but not otherwise. Changes of policy often involved much compromise by management but once policy was agreed then representatives would back the managerial decisions necessary to implement such policies. Most managers came to realize that the existence of policies agreed in this way provided them with an area over which they could, without serious question, exercise authority. The extent of this authority was recognized to be greater than that of managers in other concerns which had not initiated participation in policy making.

The negotiating institutions required within employment hierarchies

It is one thing to discuss participation in principle as I have so far done in this chapter, but it is more difficult to describe the form and detailed functions of the institutions required to give effect to participation.

Insufficient analytical thinking has been done about the various circumstances within which groups of people make decisions and the various means used by such groups in arriving at decisions. Because Parliament makes its decisions by majority vote, majority voting is often regarded as the only manner in which a group of persons can make a decision. And yet buried within the ambit of terms such as consultation and negotiation are a range of methods of taking decisions which have not been described in defined terms. Before discussing participation further I propose to describe these methods.

Some definitions

First I shall have to define the meaning I attach to some terms in order to make the meaning of what I write quite clear.

Power. Those qualities of a person or an association of persons that enable him or them to cause other persons to act.

Authority. That quality of a role, or a group of roles, which authorizes the person occupying the role to make decisions and act within defined limits. (The connection between power and authority arises from the fact that those with power can endow roles with authority.)

Association. A voluntary coming together of people who share common objectives and are prepared to accept some common rules of behaviour to achieve them. (An association is one type of institution.) Examples of associations are shareholders of a company, members of a club, members of a Trade Union, staff of a department of a company who elect representatives, members of professional institutions, members of a students' union of a university or members of its teaching staff.

The nature of committees

When members of an association wish to have their affairs managed for them they elect representatives and these representatives form a committee.

The task of the committee is to make decisions which are felt by committee members to be in the best interests of the association and which are in accord with the wishes of the greatest number of its members. The members of the committee can do no more than exert their personal power of persuasion over each other. No committee members (formally at least) have a special relationship with a particular sector of the association because each committee member has been elected by a process of voting in which *all* members of the association took part. In other words each committee member is chosen by a majority of members of the association.

The 'wholeness' of the association which is manifest in the process of election has the result that no single member of the committee represents a particular group within the association from which he might derive power over other members of the committee.*

I shall refer to such an association as a '*simple association*' and to the body which they elect as a 'committee'. These are the conditions under which the body of representatives makes its decisions by majority voting. Figure 5 depicts a committee.

Unstable committees

But some associations take a different form when they contain a series of sub-associations each of which elects its own representatives on to a committee. I shall use the term 'constituency' to refer to these sub-associations. The members of these different constituencies share the overall objectives of the association but

---

* I have not discussed committees such as sub-committees, advisory committees, etc., which are appointed rather than elected. Almost invariably, as in the case of elected committees, they carry corporate accountability and reach their decisions by majority vote. But members of advisory committees usually have the right to submit minority reports.

There are many bodies which are called 'committees' which in my opinion are not committees. The inter-departmental 'committees' of the civil service are not committees because they cannot recommend to Ministers unless they are unanimous. Many managers describe their meetings with their immediate subordinates as 'committees', but accountability for all decisions rests on the manager not on the 'committee'.

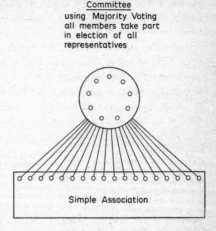

COMMITTEE: A body of representatives elected by all members of an association which carries corporate responsibility and makes its decisions by majority vote

SIMPLE ASSOCIATIONS: Those which do not contain sub-associations or separate constituencies for the election of representatives

Committee
using Majority Voting all members take part in election of all representatives

Simple Association

FIGURE 5   Committee

each constituency also has subsidiary aims and objectives. I shall refer to such associations as 'complex associations'.

A common example of a complex association is a club wherein there are different constituencies devoted to, say, golf, tennis, and social affairs. Other examples are the members of a Trade Union within a factory which elects a committee from a series of departmental constituencies or the student associates, full members, and fellows of a technological institution.

I have referred to the bodies elected by these complex associations as committees but they are, in fact, what I prefer to call 'unstable' committees. The reasons for their instability are as follows.

All the members of the complex association share overall objectives but each constituency has sub-objectives. If these sub-objectives are threatened by the majority vote of the committee, then the sub-objectives of one of the constituencies may become more important to the members of that constituency than the overall objectives of the association. The representatives of the threatened constituency will then attempt to discard majority voting because it is oppressive to them and resort to the use of power. If they have the support of their constituency they may endanger the cohesion of the complex association by obstructive tactics or even by threatening to lead the members of their constituency out of the association. When this stage is reached majority voting in the 'committee' is no longer accepted and if there is a desire to maintain the cohesion of the association, then negotiation begins. At least temporarily the body of representatives ceases to be a committee and becomes a negotiating body. Figure 6 depicts an unstable committee.

UNSTABLE COMMITTEE:
A body of representatives elected by a complex association (see below) which carries corporate responsibility and makes decisions by majority vote until the individual objectives of the sub-associations become more important than the total interests of the association. It will then start negotiating instead of majority voting

COMPLEX ASSOCIATIONS:
Those which contain sub-associations or separate constituencies for the election of representatives

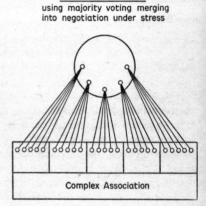

Unstable Committee
using majority voting merging
into negotiation under stress

Complex Association

FIGURE 6   Unstable Committee

Multilateral Negotiation takes place when the representatives of a number of associations meet together in an attempt to agree upon some common action, or to fuse together, or to agree a common policy, or to agree on a single bargain. But there are three identifiably different circumstances within which multilateral negotiations can take place. I will name and define these three situations and then discuss each in turn:

Simple Negotiation where if one or more associations contract out of the negotiation, then the others can proceed to agreement (Figure 7).

Complex Negotiation where it is necessary for all the associations concerned to agree or else no agreement can be reached among any of them.

Requisite Negotiation where not only must representatives of all the associations agree if a decision is to be reached but, furthermore, the circumstances of the negotiation make it essential that some change is agreed; in other words, agreement is a requirement of the situation.

Simple negotiation

The conditions surrounding simple negotiation are those often, though erroneously, assumed to apply to all negotiation. Three or four Trade Unions believe that there are possible grounds for amalgamation and they meet to see if terms can be agreed. There is no pressure on any of them to agree some particular set of terms, except self-interest. They may all feel that amalgamation is not possible. Or three of them can agree on terms and the fourth contracts out of the negotiation and goes its own way. There are very numerous examples of associations, or individuals for that matter, getting together to agree on common action and either all

SIMPLE NEGOTIATION:
Where unanimous agreement between the parties is not necessary because some of them can come to an agreement whilst others opt out

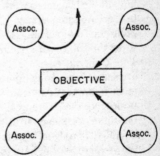

Simple Negotiation where agreement to proceed can involve some associations whilst others contract out

FIGURE 7 Simple Negotiation

51

failing to agree or some of them coming to agreement while the others fail to do so.

Complex Negotiation

There are many circumstances where all must agree or agreement is impossible between any of the associations. These are commonly concerned with situations where unco-ordinated unilateral decisions by a number of different associations are leading to situations which are detrimental to the members of all the associations. Complex negotiation seems nearly always to be concerned with the acceptance of a curtailment of the individual freedom of the associations to act alone. If one association cannot agree to sacrifice its freedom for the common good, then it is unlikely that any of the others can arrive at such an agreement. If they did so it would entail a new position where one association could continue to take decisions which were detrimental to the common good while the others would suffer the results of such decisions without having the right to retaliate. Complex negotiation is much more common than is generally recognized. Here are a number of examples:

(*a*) There are many meetings of representatives of nations (particularly at the Hague) to work out measures concerned with such matters as safety at sea, transport across national borders, pollution, radio channels, fishing limits. These measures have to be the subject of unanimous agreement.

(*b*) The General Agreement on Trade and Tariffs (GATT), arrived at between nations soon after the last war, has been a most important contributory factor to the growth of world trade since then. It represented a sacrifice by each signatory of the right to change tariffs and other conditions of trade unilaterally. The signatories to GATT, who constitute nearly all the Western World, have to agree unanimously if one country seeks to change its tariff structure in a manner which is inconsistent with the General Agreement. Whenever an apparent breach is made by one nation, very great international concern arises because the whole basis of world trade is threatened.

(c) The International Air Traffic Agreement (IATA) which sets passenger and freight rates for international air traffic, is based on unanimous agreement. It is an interesting example because recently there has been a breakdown. Had the breakdown persisted, then unregulated fare and freight competition would have resulted, but desperate efforts have been made to save the agreement, probably because it was realized that loss of revenue through open price competition might easily have led to the reduction of expenditure on maintenance and safety.

(d) There are many agreements in commerce and industry between companies concerned with such matters as uniform conditions of guarantee, standardization of specifications, safety of goods, all of which involve the sacrifice of the right to unilateral action and which consequently must apply to all competitors if agreement is to be reached.

It is increasingly being recognized that each separate association which takes part in complex negotiations has the right of veto on changes. But much difficulty could be avoided if, in every case, complex negotiation could be recognized for what it is and the requirement of unanimous consent or unanimous toleration of change, or the right of veto by each separate association (and all these mean the same), could be explicitly stated in constitutional form. We ought all to be as familiar with the behaviour expected of us in complex negotiation as we are when we join a committee. Figure 8 depicts Complex Negotiation.

Requisite Negotiation

The difference between Complex and Requisite Negotiation is this: in complex negotiation agreement has to be reached unanimously or there is no agreement. But the associations involved can tolerate failure to agree. They are not seriously damaged by lack of agreement, they merely fail to make some possible advance. The necessity for *requisite* negotiation arises where there is a combination of associations linked together in some economic, political, or social framework, to pursue different paths towards a common end. Each association depends for the fulfilment of its

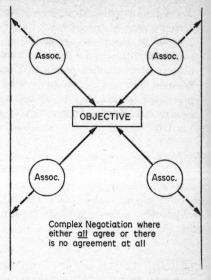

COMPLEX NEGOTIATION:
Where unanimous agreement
amongst the parties is
essential if any agreement is
to be arrived at. Opting out
by some parties makes
action by the others
impossible

Assoc.

Assoc.

OBJECTIVE

Assoc.

Assoc.

Complex Negotiation where
either _all_ agree or there
is no agreement at all

FIGURE 8   Complex Negotiation

own particular objectives not only on its own success but also on
the success of the whole combination of associations. But the
combination depends for its success on a continuous ability of all
the associations to agree changes made necessary by changes in
the economic or political environment within which the combination exists. Thus, unanimous agreement on changes is, in the long
term, essential for the continued success or even the survival of
the associations involved. Here are examples of situations where
there is a continuous need to agree change by unanimous vote.

The European Economic Community is the most dramatic
example. Its constitution provides that for certain vital questions
unanimous agreement is required. But it is clearly recognized that
continuous failure to agree will destroy the cohesion of the Community. Each country recognizes that it is not possible for the
Community to decide to stand still and rest upon its laurels
because new problems created by events outside the control of all
of its members continually arise and, unless these are solved,

disintegration will start. For example, devaluation of the French currency and later revaluation of the German currency, brought about by irresistible international financial pressures, forced both countries to breach the Common Market agricultural policy. It became essential to get unanimous agreement to the form of such breaches and this was eventually achieved after much compromise. Unanimously agreed changes are, therefore, essential for its continuance. Figure 9 depicts Requisite Negotiation.

REQUISITE NEGO-
TIATION: Where the
different associations
involved are interdep-
endent and failure to
agree regularly on
changes damages the
interest of all. In such
cases not only is
unanimous agreement
necessary if action is
to be taken but
changes are essential

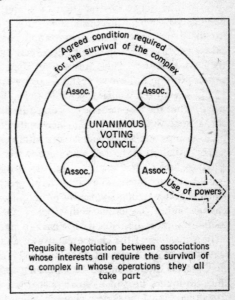

Requisite Negotiation between associations whose interests all require the survival of a complex in whose operations they all take part

FIGURE 9   Requisite Negotiation

Requisite Negotiation in industry

The most common example of requisite negotiation occurs in industrial companies. As I have already commented, companies are an example of combinations of associations of shareholders, represented by the board of directors; the company's customers (an amorphous association whose interest has to be represented by sales managers because they do not elect representatives), and representatives of different Trade Unions, different departments, or different strata of employees. These representatives may represent simple or complex associations. Changes have to be made if the company is to be able to continue to employ people on satisfactory conditions to satisfy the market and to make profits. Unless agreement to such changes is obtained the company will eventually fail. Furthermore, because the company's existence involves the active co-operation of shareholders, who supply capital, customers, who consume the output, and employees, who do the daily work of the organization, each one of them has power because they can disrupt the organization by withdrawing their co-operation. Thus, any one of these groups may use its power position or its legal authority to try to influence the others to agree with the changes which it seeks. There is thus a great need for all the associations concerned in the work of an industrial company to be very clear indeed about the nature of their relationships and the circumstances within which they negotiate.

The situation is that all who have power or authority in the situation must agree change. They do it tacitly if it is of little importance to them. They may have previously authorized a general policy giving somebody in authority the right to make change within the terms of that policy. Or they may, on new issues of importance, specifically have to state their approval.

In a meeting of the chief executive of a company with representatives of its employees, the situation is somewhat more complex than is often assumed because the company's shareholders and customers are, in a sense, also represented by the chief executive. He cannot agree changes which he believes might be rejected by the board or the shareholders or cause extensive loss of business from customers. The chief executive must take his decisions in negotiation in accordance with explicit or assumed terms of reference which he believes will be acceptable to these two power groups. Likewise, representatives who are members of Trade Unions have to bear in mind the policies of those unions as well as the interest of those who elected them. Thus each of the associations involved in, say, a manufacturing company has a choice. It can either go on compromising with the others until all are agreed, or it can risk trying to use its power to force the others to accept what it wants. By taking the latter course it puts the entire combination of associations at risk.

Participation depends on clear negotiating institutions

This degree of understanding of the nature of the institutions within which negotiations of various kinds take place is, I believe, basic to the whole idea of participation. Without explicit structuring* and understanding of the rules of behaviour which necessarily apply in given situations, those who want to progress amicably and constructively towards agreement do not know how to deal with regressive or destructive behaviour on the part of others. Where there are no explicit rules everybody is driven to the use of the lowest common denominator of counter-productive tactics.

I have suggested earlier that the essence of what employees want when they use the phrase 'more participation' is the right one to take a 'full part' in deciding the policies within which the enterprise is managed. In the event I found† that this was narrowed down by employees' representatives to the taking of a 'full part' in the formulation of these policies which bear directly on working conditions. Policies which affected relations between the company's shareholders or its customers, although of interest to and often discussed by representatives, were not matters in which they desired to intervene unless a by-product of such policies had a direct bearing on conditions of employment.

Conditions of Participation

If employees and their representatives are to be able to feel that their aspirations to take a 'full part' in the formulation of policies are fulfilled, then the following conditions have not only to exist but have to be plainly seen to exist:

1. New policies or change in policies must not be introduced without the agreement of the representatives of all those affected.

* See the Appendix for details of the institutions required.
† During twenty-five years' experience of operating unanimous voting councils in The Glacier Metal Co. Ltd.

2. Representatives of any Union, department, or stratum of employees in an employment institution must each have the right to veto changes until conditions have been agreed which will render these at least tolerable to the people they represent.

3. Until changes are agreed, then the *status quo* must continue to operate.

4. Management must also have, by agreement, the right to veto any changes proposed by representatives.

5. When new policies are agreed they must be carefully written and continuously available to all employees for reference.

6. Managers must be trained not only in the formal content of agreed policies but also in the spirit in which they are to be interpreted.

7. An explicit and formal appeal procedure must be set up so that managerial decisions which appear to contradict the letter or spirit of those policies are delayed until reviewed by successive higher levels of managerial authority.

Given the achievement of such conditions then I believe that a number of changes will take place:

(*a*) most employees will accept the authority of managers to make such decisions as seem appropriate to the efficient running of the organization as long as those decisions are consistent with agreed policies.

(*b*) employees' representatives will be much more reluctant to resort to the use of power.

(*c*) a feeling of participation on the part of most employees will develop as they begin to trust the efficacy of the new institutions.

These are not new proposals to give effect to the cry for more participation. Together with others I have been advocating them for many years.* They represent no sacrifice of managerial authority as compared with existing circumstances. Indeed, if implemented, managers would, in my experience, find themselves

* My book, *Exploration in Management* (Heinemann Educational Books and Penguin Books) contains full details of my proposals for participation. My more recent book *Organization* (*op. cit.*) delves still more deeply into the subject.

with secure usable authority within an area of discretion bounded by agreed policies.

This would be a very notable accretion of authority compared to the current situation of many managers who never know when any decision which they make is going to be challenged by representatives backed by the threat of banning overtime, working to rule, refusing co-operation, or striking.

Furthermore, if by joint agreement a unanimous-voting council is set up and all its members come to recognize that they are dealing with 'Requisite Negotiation' as I have defined it earlier, then a new position will have been established. Not only will employees' representatives have the constitutional right to veto change (which they already have in unconstitutional form owing to their power to strike) but management too will possess this right of veto so long as the constitution is adhered to.

The results of setting up a unanimous-voting council

Structured participation based on unanimous-voting councils (one could call them Power-equating Councils) will produce a range of results:

(a) At first it will prove slow work to get agreement on changes to policies. Representatives will test the integrity of managers' agreement not to change policy without unanimous agreement by holding up changes simply in order to see what happens.

(b) Managers will have to agree unpalatable compromises in order to get any agreement. They should remember when this occurs that they would in any case have been unable to implement the full changes which they desired without building up a feeling of hostility which would have led to the next outburst of conflict.

(c) When changes in policy have been agreed, managers will find they have a high degree of authority from representatives to take decisions towards the implementation of those changes.

(d) Representatives will gradually cease to threaten the use of their power of disruption when they realize that they have constitutional and peaceful means of preventing unwanted changes instead of having to resort to expensive power tactics.

(e) The deliberations of the council will produce a series of explicit internal policies within which managers have full authority to make decisions. This will reduce very greatly the time spent by representatives and managers in negotiating over the same issues time and again as they arise. One agreed written policy can save hundreds of hours of irritable argument over many years to come.

(f) The real importance of representatives as 'legislators' along with management will have been established. The proper feeling of their own importance will be enhanced. Their fantasies about the 'authoritarian' character of management will be reduced.

(g) Those who elect representatives will gradually realize that constitutional power* now rests in the hands of their representatives and that constant consideration of disruptive action to constrain managers is no longer necessary. A feeling of real participation will begin to grow.

The Appendix sets out the details of the constitution of a unanimous-voting council.

*.The thoughts of some will turn to questions such as 'Will this constitutional power be used to prevent an essential measure of redundancy or the essential closing of a factory?' In my experience, councils can handle such issues. I have discussed such issues at length in *Organization* (*op. cit.*).

CHAPTER 6

The right to abundant employment

In the presence of the very high recent levels of unemployment, a
feeling of what might be described as hopelessness seems to be
developing in our society. Ever more people are talking about the
inevitability of serious unemployment. There is talk of reduced
working hours and earlier retirement as a means of alleviation
of the situation caused by increasing automation, mechanization, and computerization.

Those who lived in the 1920s and 1930s will recognize the
similarity between the views now being expressed and those
which were much more widely prevalent in those early years.
The anxieties, to which I have already referred, about the
increasing number of people who will be condemned to 'boring
button-pushing jobs' coupled with this increasing gloom about
the inevitability of continued serious unemployment, is throwing
a psychological shadow over the whole of the employment zone.

In Chapter 2 I attempted to demonstrate that the 'more and
more boring jobs' gloom was false and that in fact the long-term
prospect is the opposite. But I did point out that in the presence
of unemployment many people are forced to accept roles where
the level of personal capacity of the people involved is well above
that required to do the work. In other words, unemployment
causes over-manning* of jobs on a serious scale. I also pointed
out that because human capacity increases with age (see Figure
3) that if opportunity for change of job involving gradual
degrees of promotion is denied because of unemployment, then
the jobs of millions of people may become boring and unsatisfactory to them.

It would seem, therefore, that if it were possible effectively to
solve the problem of unemployment we should not only remove

---

* I have used the term over-manning to describe the situation where the
capacity of the person is above that required for the work on which he is
employed.

the fear of actual loss of job but also ensure the prospect of more interesting work for most people.

Fifty years ago many believed that job insecurity was one of the essential stimulants which caused people to do 'a decent day's work' and that the converse feeling of being assured of employment caused indiscipline and laxity.

This always seemed to me to be an absurd notion and today I think most of us realize that anything which produces anxiety or fear in the individual also gives rise to hostility, unreasonableness, reduced performance, and ill-health.

Abundant employment must be one of the major goals of our society if we are to have any hope of curing the current ills of the employment zone. I have used the term abundant employment and must explain what meaning I attach to it.

Abundant employment is a situation where every member of the working population has a fair opportunity to use his personal capacity to the full extent which he desires on work which interests him and which enables him to earn a wage or salary which is consistent with the earnings of others doing a similar level of work to himself.

'*Full employment*' *is not enough*

'Full employment' is usually interpreted to mean a national situation where the total number of vacant jobs is higher than the number of those unemployed. Full employment has been a target in our society since the War and from time to time it has been achieved. But even when it is achieved it does not provide abundant employment in accordance with my definition. Within conditions of full employment there always have been areas of the country or specific types of occupation or age groups where job opportunity is seriously lacking. That is bad enough if we are looking at the employment zone from a human and social point of view. But if we get two or three per cent of unemployment, then not only are large numbers deprived of jobs but millions of others are tied by feelings of insecurity to tasks which they dislike or to work which fails to use their capacity to the full.

As I have already said, the ability of people changes as they mature. If any of us are denied the opportunity to get a job which contains a level of work reasonably consistent with our changing ability either by promotion or by change from one employer to another, then we become bored, frustrated, and eventually aggrieved by the society in which we live. If enough people are put into a situation which gives rise to this attitude of mind, then the employment zone becomes a battle-ground of 'we' against 'them'.

Re-emerging fears about the apparent insolubility of the problem of unemployment and the unjustified but real gloom about the effects of automation, use of computers, etc., are some of the causes of the extremely unhappy industrial relations which are upon us. I believe it to be very difficult for some people with secure incomes and relatively secure jobs to realize the extent of the havoc created by this particular form of insecurity. We all know it is an evil to be dealt with but too often tend to submerge our concern in the thought that unemployed persons can at least exist on social payments. But if we comfort ourselves in this way we forget the long-term bitterness which periods of unemployment create even after return to work, and also the loss of security and career opportunity which affects millions who are not actually unemployed.

Established Civil Servants are virtually assured of continuous employment until retirement age. This is possible because of the need for an apparently steady increase in their numbers because the total number employed is some 500,000 and because when some employees are no longer required in one sector they can be transferred to another. The spectre of redundancy does not arise.* This enviable situation cannot be achieved in industry or commerce because the activity of concerns fluctuates widely. The equivalent of forced transfer from one Civil Service sector to another in industry is redundancy leading to the taking of a post in another concern. I cannot see abundant employment leading to a cessation of all redundancy situations. But so long as alternative positions containing similar levels of work at similar

* Though individuals can be prematurely retired on fairly generous terms, on grounds of lack of suitability or in special cases of redundancy.

wages or salaries are available then the worst features of redundancy will have been removed.

There is the problem that a very small minority seem to prefer to exist on social security benefits. This problem is grossly magnified by some who comment upon it. But it seems folly to me to worry too much about perhaps a few thousand who decline work when it is offered, when hundreds of thousands who desperately want work cannot get it.

Social priorities must come first

Dr Tom Bier, an American sociologist who is at present a consultant to a very large British company, gave a salutary warning in a recent lecture.

He pointed out that seventy years of concentration on economic efficiency in the United States had been carried out in a way which constituted an exploitation of human and social values; that Britain was in many ways a better place in which to live today precisely because we had not in the past followed this path so zealously as the United States and some other nations. He went on to suggest that we in Britain were now feeling so guilty about our comparative economic failure that, just at the point where others were at last beginning to realize the need to change their priorities, Britain appeared to be hell-bent on asserting the supremacy of economic goals. He suggested that this was likely to make our lives less rather than more satisfactory!

I agree with Dr Bier but would add a rider to what he says. Further increase in economic efficiency is being retarded because we give such low priority to human affairs. This is one of the modern paradoxes. Now that we have reached, in Britain, an age of potential plenty, the priorities of the man in the street are changing: status, relationships, liberty, freedom from anxiety, security, and health, have become more important than material standards of living. It is the absence of national plans giving due priority to such matters that is harmful to our economic performance. We damage the latter by giving it too much priority. By analogy, we are like a man who wants to achieve high esteem publicly: if he bends every effort to displaying his own virtue he will fail in his objective.

If we could agree to go hell-bent for human values at work we might well get the economic efficiency we need as a by-product. But the converse doesn't work. If we put great emphasis on economic efficiency we destroy human values.

I don't think there is much which I have written in this chapter so far which differs from the aspirations of most people. The argument starts only when we come to discussing the means of achieving the ends we agree upon: many people will agree the ends without agreeing the means of getting there.

People are the source of wealth

Apparently many people in society have not appreciated or have forgotten some very simple axioms. If everybody in society who wants to work has a job; if the techniques in use are reasonably efficient, and if the equipment available is reasonably up to date, then we are producing wealth at about our maximum potential. But if equipment is not up to date and if we have a million un-employed, then we are wasting our potential.

Thus to suggest that 'we shall never again be able to employ our whole working population fully because of automation and computers' is dangerous nonsense. The fact is that the availability of very large numbers of people without employment who want to work is a situation of great potential for increase of living standards.

Furthermore if we have in employment large numbers whose personal ability fits them for carrying out higher-level work than their existing jobs provide, then that too is a situation of frustration for the present but also one of great potentiality for improving the economic performance of society.

I am diffident about hammering away at these truisms but it seems to be necessary because attitudes developing on the part of increasing numbers of people seem to deny them.

People talk about the German economic miracle but what is seldom pointed out is that one of the important factors was the large supply of labour available. This supply came from immigration from Eastern Germany, from an influx of labour from other countries, and from a transfer of people from agriculture to industry. (Germany still employs over ten per cent of its working population in agriculture, whereas the British figure is about two and a half per cent.) Thus one of the big factors in the German economic success was the availability of people for employment. Similar situations have held in Japan and in France.

I refer to these other countries simply to reinforce the point that you cannot create wealth without people and that a million unemployed, though a current social tragedy, is a future economic potential for increase in wealth for all.

We tend to debate these great issues in terms of money when we ought to debate them in terms of the availability of people to get the jobs done. Have we enough people to create a great expansion in the building programme so that the rocketing price of housing can be halted and then reduced? The answer is that of course we have and therefore such expansion is possible. But when we turn to the detail we are involved in the whole gamut of housing financial policy, subsidies, taxation, and like issues. These issues have to be faced in terms, for example, of higher taxation of incomes or more widespread use of compulsory purchase of land. But if we jib at such things, then we are willing the ends and denying the means. The creation of abundant employment is not in principle a problem. The problem arises simply over the means; and as long as individually or collectively we reject the methods of getting rid of unemployment because it impinges marginally on our own incomes, or because the planned housing estate might spoil our country paradise, or because we don't want a convalescent home for mental patients in our road, or because expanding the production capacity of our company in a development area means living in a less attractive area of the country, then we are rejecting abundant employment.

If we don't all make up our minds that in the interests of abundant employment we must all put up with personal disadvantages arising from the means required to create that situation then we shall all suffer grievously in the future. The growing unrest which we can see every evening on our television screens is an ominous sign that the employment zone is going to be a scene of ever-growing chaos if we do not all resolutely determine to agree the means of creating abundant employment.

Why have we not achieved abundant employment?

Governments of all political complexions in all industrialized countries have been fearful of abundant employment for two main reasons. The first is based on the assumption that full employment or over-employment (as many people would call what I mean by abundant employment) inevitably leads to unacceptable rates of wage inflation. The second reason is linked to the first. High rates of wage inflation lead (*a*) to a rapid rise in consumption with consequential increases in imports and (*b*) to a rapid rise in prices which make a country's exports uncompetitive in price. These conditions lead to deficits on the balance of payments and force countries to devalue their currencies. In an attempt to inhibit this chain of events governments take steps to 'reduce activity in the economy' by measures such as reducing the supply of money and credit, reducing government capital investment and expenditure on the social services, and increasing the taxes on incomes and goods. If these economic measures are successful in their aim of reducing national consumption they inevitably lead to the emergence of unemployment. Thus every government wants to maintain full employment but is usually 'driven off-course by economic factors beyond our control' and as a result we do not get consistent full employment.

But there is a flaw in the thinking which leads up to this cycle of events. The assumption that it is full employment which causes wage inflation is no longer correct, if indeed it ever was. The level of employment and the rate of wage inflation are today independent variables. This is clearly demonstrated by what happened in 1971. In that year we had the maximum rate of unemployment since 1939, coinciding with the maximum rate of wage inflation this century. Slightly less dramatic instances of the simultaneous existence of high unemployment and high wage inflation have occurred many times since the War. The same applies to 1972. If one bases one's actions on a theory that if x goes up, y must come down and vice versa, and one is faced with the fact that x and y consistently rise simultaneously, then surely it is complete folly to continue to believe in such a theory.

What has been evident since 1945 but not faced by many economists, Treasury officials, Chancellors of the Exchequer, and governments, is that the rate of wage inflation in various industries and sectors of the employment zone is a function of the power of various Trade Unions to disrupt the company, the industry, or the country, if their claims for higher earnings are not met.

The vicious circle

The extent to which different Trade Unions are prepared to use their power is of course dependent on many factors such as the cost of living, industrial profits, the degree of co-operation they are receiving from management or from the government itself in many directions and, perhaps most important of all, the feelings of their members at work in the factories and elsewhere. If people in employment are feeling critical about the level of their earnings compared to that of others; anxious about the security of their jobs; critical of management because of feelings of lack of participation in the formation of the policies which govern their working conditions; devoid of easy means of challenging managerial decisions which they feel to be improper; then one way of expressing themselves is to demand that their Union leaders use their power to insist on large increases in earnings.

Thus do we achieve a sort of vicious circle. Insecurity generated by unemployment and lack of attention to the human factors in employment lead to large wage claims. These lead to rising consumption and cause the government to try to slow down the economy by reducing demand. This leads to more unemployment.

Breaking the vicious circle

As soon as it is accepted that the level of employment and the rate of wage inflation are independent of each other, then it becomes obvious that the attempt to control wage inflation and the consequent rise in consumption by reducing the level of activity in the economy is by and large counter-productive. On the whole attempts to follow such a course have in fact made matters worse rather than better. But facing up to the facts in this way does not, of itself, provide a solution to the problem. If it is accepted that the level of employment and the rate of wage inflation are independent variables, then separate measures must be introduced to deal with each. We can no longer hope, even if it were desirable, to control wage inflation indirectly by slowing down or hotting up the level of employment and the level of activity in the economy.

We must therefore move forward to a situation where the economy is stimulated to run at full blast continuously, and simultaneously introduce democratic means whereby wage and salary levels do not run amok. If, in addition, we also introduce other changes in the employment zones which I have discussed in previous chapters then we shall stimulate psychological changes in the attitude of people to work, which will relieve social tensions, reduce hostility, and increase national wealth.

If, therefore, unemployment is to be abolished and abundant employment maintained in its place, it is necessary to create means, and they must be democratic means, of controlling wage * inflation within bounds set by Parliament. We must do this in such a manner as to bring about gradually a realignment of the pattern of differential earnings which will produce a more acceptable relation between wages and the level of work done.

In my last two chapters to follow, I shall therefore set out proposals for reversing the current trend towards differential wages which are a function of power, and moving towards equitable wages.

* From here onwards, whenever I use the term 'wages' I refer to the earnings of all types of employees without exception. I also include in the term, earnings, such things as holidays, pensions, hours of work, and other fringe benefits. When I use the term labour, I refer to all types of employee from top to bottom of employment hierarchies.

CHAPTER 7

The right to equitable payment

I define equitable payment as a level of earnings for employees in different occupations which are intuitively felt by society to be reasonably consistent with the importance of the work which each does and which seem relatively fair to the individual. But before plunging into the discussion of how equitable payment is to be established, I wish to explore some of the lessons of this country's past history because I believe that they have a bearing on the current situation in the employment zone and that from them we can deduce the action which is necessary today.

Basis of the acceptance of the law

In the early days of our history, law was accepted on the basis of custom as affected by the interaction of the crown, the church, and the magnates, the minor lords and the townsmen having marginal claims to consideration. In Magna Carta we see the assertion of the rights of individuals, or at least of important individuals, against the crown, and also of the authority of a numerical majority to decide the policy of the body on which they served – this latter not being automatically clear in those days. The development of Parliament gave the lesser gentry and the chartered townsfolk a clearer place within the political classes, and extended the idea of constitutional power rather than the use of physical or psychological force.

By the end of the eighteenth century, however, there was an outrageous discrepancy between the 'political' society represented in Parliament, and the economic and social basis of the nation. In the face of tradition, and the awful example of the French Revolution, the struggle for Parliamentary reform was long and arduous, and pursued to the verge of insurrection. In the last resort, the public demand was met by the Reform Act of 1832. A generation later, demands for extension of the franchise were met with comparative speed and the merest shadow of violence. Thus manual operatives came into the political classes. The next extension of the franchise was a comparatively humdrum affair, but brought the country close to manhood suffrage, which has been attained in this century, and extended to teenagers of eighteen. On the other hand, votes for women, though finally granted without difficulty, were another matter of acute controversy, overshadowed by violence and threats of violence.

The prevailing rule has been, that in modern times changes have been granted when backed by a great force of public opinion, even though this did not have the levers of legal power in its hands.

I am no historian but here are some extracts from the writing of H. A. L. Fisher* on the first great movement of reform:

1. 'Even the Duke of Wellington, the sternest of Tories, was prepared in the end to assent to Parliamentary Reform. The age of Metternich is not then a period of immobility in the domestic history of England. On the contrary, it is one in which great measures were passed, and great changes sanctioned, exhibiting the growing liberality of the English political mind. Trade unions were legalized in 1824, the tariff simplified in 1826. First the Protestant dissenters were admitted to office, then the Catholics to the vote. Finally, the Reform Act of 1832, passed in response to an overwhelming body of opinion in the country, enfranchised the middle class, liberated the House of Commons from aristocratic control and led by a natural sequence to the democratization of town government. . . .'

2. 'The English did not look far ahead. Great risks were run and much suffering was caused through deference to vested interests and unchecked economic appetites. But in the moments of real emergency the right action was taken. When revolution threatened, the middle class was admitted to power.'

The social battles of that period centred around the extension of the franchise. If it was delayed then the groups who sought it

* *A History of Europe*, Vol. II. Fontana.

used their power to disrupt. Those who were denied constitutional authority resorted to power instead.

No doubt many people of that age were deploring the breakdown of the rule of law just as so many do today in the face of disruption by various Trade Unions. But as Fisher remarks, a great Tory Minister such as Sir Robert Peel 'was capable of adjusting his principles to the lesson of facts'. The question which arises for us today is 'are we capable of adjusting our principles to the lesson of current facts?'

The British legislature is now based on about as wide a distribution of the franchise as is possible but what must be noted is that all members of Parliament are elected by *geographical* constituencies.

Change in the basis of the franchise required

But the great power groups in society who remain unrepresented are *occupational* groups. They, as such, are totally unrepresented. We talk of 'Trade Union M.P.s' but this is a myth. A representative is one who is elected to concern himself with the interests of those who elected him and who can be withdrawn by electors. So called 'Trade Union M.P.s' are those who receive a contribution to their constituency expenses from a Trade Union. But they cannot be withdrawn by that Trade Union. Indeed if a Trade Union threatens to cease its contribution in order to pressurize an M.P. into voting in some particular direction, it is liable to be arraigned by Parliament.

The result of this situation is that Parliament throughout this century has been extremely diffident about trying to introduce law which directly affects earnings in the employment zone. Parliament knows intuitively, if not consciously, that legislation which directly affects groups which are not represented in the legislature is likely to be resisted by the use of power and that in the disruption which follows the law will be brought into contempt.

The 1971 Industrial Relations Act does not in fact impinge seriously on earnings nor does it countervail the power of Trade Unions, for by following a few simple rules the Trade Unions remain as powerful as they have been. But the vigorous resentment to the Act arose, I think, from a deep-seated instinct that this is legislation without representation. One of the most stupid acts of the 1970 Conservative government was the offer to discuss the proposed Bill with the T.U.C. *but subject to the proviso that they were not prepared to alter any of the principles contained in their proposals*. This was indeed imposition. The angry response and the use of power to try to prevent the operation of the Act was predictable. I hear, behind all the shouting, the cry 'No legislation without representation'.

We have a constitutional problem

There is in my opinion a widespread failure to realize the true nature of the current problem. It is constitutional by nature. Winston Churchill in his Romanes lectures given in the 1930s recognized this when he proposed a third House of Parliament which he called 'the House of Industry'. I do not agree with his proposals because the House was to be composed of employers and employees and they were to be appointed, not elected. Nevertheless the germ of the idea was there.

Our current problem can be solved only by some institution the members of which shall be elected by occupational power groups. Such representation of people in their widely varied role as employees who can take a proper part in the formation of legislation which directly impinges on the employment zone is, I believe, inevitable if we are to solve our problems. As I write the government, the C.B.I., and the T.U.C. are engaged in negotiation concerned with means of solving these problems. Some agreement may soon emerge. But I believe the results of any agreement will be temporary only unless they are based on a realistic appreciation of the constitutional nature of the problem. We are again faced, as we were so often in the nineteenth century, with the need to extend the franchise – but to extend it in a manner which has no historical precedent. At the end of this chapter I shall propose the establishment of a new institution which would bring this about. First, however, I must present an analysis of the situation in which we find ourselves.

'Free bargaining' over wages

Most governments in the Western World remain firmly committed to the notion that the varying wage pattern from one occupation to another and from one industry to another should result from a process of free bargaining between employers and representatives of employees. Many people assume that it is the only possible way to settle differential wages.

But it may greatly surprise them to realize that there never has been free bargaining over *group* wage levels. A bargain can be defined as a contract which is entered into voluntarily by both or all parties to the negotiation. Free bargaining clearly implies the possibility of the parties to the negotiation failing to agree on a contract. One negotiates to sell one's house but if the price offered seems unsatisfactory one has not got to sell. One negotiates as an individual with a prospective employer about a job – but if the conditions offered are not satisfactory one has no necessity to take on the job.

In so called 'free bargaining' about *group* wages for existing employees there is no possibility of either the employer or the employees altogether rejecting a settlement. There may be temporary rejection manifested by a prolonged strike or lock-out. But unless the employer is prepared to close down his business and all the employees are prepared to seek jobs elsewhere, then eventually some contract about wages and conditions of work must be accepted by both parties. That is not free bargaining!

The fact is that group wages have virtually always been decided by the differential power of the employer and representatives of employees.

In the nineteenth century the power of employers was such that they were able to impose, on employees, scandalous conditions of work. Gradually the balance of power has swung until today Trade Unions possess overwhelming power based on their ability to disrupt the company, the industry, or even the nation. In the interim between these extremes the balance of power was such at times to make it appear that free bargaining was in progress. But it has always been power-dominated negotiation. The balance of power between employer and employee, not scarcity or surplus of labour, was the main factor which decided the rate of wage inflation. The market position of surplus or shortage has been a secondary factor which has influenced the power position of the two sides. But as we saw in 1971, one million unemployed certainly did not reduce the power of the Trade Unions.

The Market Theory of Wages

The second thing to notice about this false assumption of the existence of free bargaining is that it arises from the notion that the cost of labour behaves like a commodity in the market. 'Free bargaining' is a conception which historically arises out of the market-place. Bargaining implies the existence of a buyer (the employer) and a seller (the Trade Union). The whole conception can be simply referred to as the Market Theory of Wages. It operates if an individual is negotiating with an employer whether or not to accept his offer of employment. But it does not operate in relation to changes in the level of wages of groups of people already employed because neither the employer nor the employee can do without each other. It is very doubtful if the Market Theory of Wages has ever operated in such circumstances. Certainly it is not operating today.

The Market Theory was always supposed to ensure in the long run that the supply of labour for particular types of jobs was well adjusted to the demand for such labour. If there were a surplus of labour for some type of employment, then the theory assumed that wages would fall and this would dissuade some people from wishing to enter that type of employment. If there were a shortage of labour for some types of employment, then wages would rise, thus enticing more people to enter that type of employment.

But the power of Trade Uunions and professional associations is today relatively unaffected by the level of employment. They are in a situation to press their demands regardless of the extent of unemployment among their members. As a result the differential pattern of wages in the employment zone has become a function of the differential power of different Trade Unions. Those in a position to cause the most disruption to the company, the service, the industry, or the nation, command the highest wages. Those with the least power, the lowest wages.

Thus power overrides what used to be held as economic law. Take, for example, the case of dock workers. Since the advent of new methods of loading and unloading ships there has been a very large and growing surplus of dock workers. According to the market theory of wages this should have forced a decline in the wages of dockers or at least a relatively slow increase compared to others. But, in fact, despite surplus dock labour, the increase in the wages of dockers since 1967 has been higher than average. The result is that few dockers desired to leave that type of employment because they would have had to accept employment at lower wages elsewhere.

There is a nostalgic illusion which seems to be held by some economists that one day economic forces will reassert themselves and the Market Theory of Wages will once more begin to operate. I hope this will never be so. We must seek to achieve a position where any employed person is paid wages that are consistent with the level of work which he is doing regardless of whether there is surplus or shortage of the sort of skill which his ability represents.* This is what I mean when I use the phrase, 'equitable wages'.

The problem of general inflation

I have by now made it clear that I believe that the major factor in general inflation is rapidly rising wages and that this is due to

* Some may ask how important services and industries are to be manned if those in charge of them do not increase wages in order to attract the additional employees required. It is not my purpose to explore such issues in this book, but many economic mechanisms are available to government for dealing with such problems of national economic planning. For example, if, in the view of the government too many people are employed in the manufacture of, say, durable consumer goods, thus creating a shortage of people for employment in essential services, then they can gradually increase indirect taxation on consumer durables. This would increase their price in the market, reduce consumption and result in a decline in the number employed. This would produce redundancies. If there was unemployment, such redundancies would create great hardship but I am postulating the continuous future existence of full employment.

the uncounterbalanced power of Trade Unions in negotiation. But it is certainly not the only factor. There are many others such as over-investment in capital resources,* unjustified price increases, excessive profits, the psychological effect of some excessively high incomes, lack of control over land speculation, lack of savings, excessive provision of credit, and so on. But the feature of all these other causes of general inflation is that any government with the will and determination to deal with them can do so. The economic mechanisms exist in various forms of legislative action and taxation. For example, price control, though administratively arduous, is perfectly possible, excessive accumulation of private wealth can be dealt with through direct taxation of income, capital gains tax and alteration of the law to prevent people evading death duty by transferring wealth before they die.

The only point I wish to make in referring to these matters is that the governmental mechanisms for dealing with such causes of inflation exist and are understood. This is in direct contrast to the problem of wage inflation where the mechanisms are not available. Indeed, not only are means of control absent but apparently such confusion about the situation exists as to direct thought on the whole issue into schemes which are, at any rate to me, not practicable.

I will set out in my last chapter a new democratic institution which could control wage inflation and start us moving towards equitable payment for all. But I wish it to be understood that the means I suggest could only be introduced as part of a package deal. The other parts of the deal would have to contain provisions which would clearly assure employees and Trade Unions that general inflation was not to be solved simply by controlling wage levels. These other provisions would have to make it clear that the other sources of inflation would also be dealt with resolutely and at the same time.

The emphasis which I now place on resolving the problem of wage inflation arises simply because means of dealing with it are not yet available while the means for dealing with the other causes of general inflation are available.

* Though this is certainly not a factor in 1969–72, an era when private investment has been falling.

77

Wage differentials are the key factor

Demands for increased wages are largely based, not on the absolute value of what is sought, but on acute anxiety on the part of occupational groups lest they are falling behind others in the race.

All of us, as employees, are being forced, by the current situation, to defend the standard of living of our families by joining with others in the use of power. We have in recent years been forced to accept that if we are reasonable we are left behind in the differential wage race whereas militancy brings home the lolly. If we fail to combine for strength then we are left with the burden of paying, out of relatively low wages, the higher prices for everything brought about by the high wage deals forced through by others.

Current circumstances and outdated methods and institutions for dealing with these economic matters are thus forcing anti-social behaviour on a country which has been much less inclined to such behaviour than other countries for at least the past two centuries. If we are to be relieved from these anti-social pressures, then means must be created for shifting the pattern of differential wages away from one dominated by power bargaining towards one where gradually earnings more and more become a function of the differential importance to the community of the type of work being done. We need a pattern of differential earnings which seems fair to representatives of all the different types of occupation.

At present all the thousands of wage bargains are completely unco-ordinated one to the other. There is no procedure which calculates what percentage of the wage cake is used up as one employer/employee bargain after another is struck. There is no authority presiding over the process which seeks to ensure that the pattern of differential wages between one occupation and another bears any relationship to the importance of the work which each carries out. The result is that our national pattern of differential wages is beginning to reflect not some felt and agreed equitable pattern but the differential power of the bargaining groups. Most to the strongest – least to the weakest. Can we really continue to countenance a situation where some dockers are paid more than twice as much as many teachers and young doctors? There are many such examples of gross inequity.

Wage Control Methods which have failed

1. *Productivity-based wages.* Many believe that wage levels ought to be related to productivity and over the past ten years many deals granting increased wages have been concluded, ostensibly, on this basis. Piece-work and other forms of direct monetary incentives are one form of productivity deals. Industry is at last realizing the folly of such payment systems and is moving on to payment of hourly rates or weekly salaries. I shall not explore the shortcomings of such systems for I have already done so at length elsewhere.*

Governments have promoted the idea that employers should offer higher wages to Trade Unions against guarantees of higher output and elimination of restrictive practices. But these have in general failed. The problems associated with such an approach are as follows:

(*a*) There is no current means in use of measuring a mixed output of work. Thus to offer a ten per cent wage increase for a five per cent increase in output when it is not possible to measure output at all is absurd.†

(*b*) Even if we could measure a mixed output we are unable to determine how much of that increase is due to the efforts of the employees who are to be rewarded, how much is due to

---

* See *Piecework Abandoned*, Wilfred Brown (Heinemann Educational Books Ltd).

† I am well aware that most people and companies assume that output is measurable but this is not so. Added value as a parameter of output varies with market prices. Adding up the costs of a mixed output involves the grave error of using *inputs* to measure *outputs*. We cannot take the physical volume or weight of output if that output is composed of a mix of different products. A method of measurement has in fact been devised and is described in certain chapters of *Organization* (*op. cit.*) and there is a more extensive treatment of the technique in *Product Analysis Pricing*, Wilfred Brown and Elliott Jaques (Heinemann Educational Books Ltd).

the efforts of others in developing new techniques of production and how much is due to the installation of new and more efficient plant.

(c) Even if we could surmount the two previously mentioned hurdles we would find ourselves in an impossible situation. We would be paying more to people who had held back production in the past by employee protective practices* and who, by elimination of such practices, could produce more. But we would be refusing to pay more to those who had not employed such practices in the past and could not therefore necessarily increase output in the future.

(d) Finally the conception of productivity-regulated wages does not take account of the differential level of work being done by individual members of groups of employees. All work involves decision-taking within defined areas. This is what we pay for – decisions! The level of importance of the decisions vary greatly from role to role. Design draughtsmen take more important decisions than those who detail their drawings.† Managers have to make more important decisions than their subordinates. Many, perhaps most, jobs have no physical output at all. For example, the service industries and the Civil Service.

Thus even if we could surmount all the difficulties inherent in productivity wage deals which I have described, such a basis of trying to establish a pattern of equitable wages is not applicable in a very large proportion of jobs.

2. *Government-imposed wages*. These have generally taken the form of setting a ceiling in percentage terms above which wages cannot legally be increased for a stated period. Their effect is to freeze differentials which is highly unsatisfactory. In any case it is generally acknowledged that though such measures may be necessary as a short-term expedient to counter an economic

* I prefer the phrase 'employee protective practices' to the more generally used 'restrictive practices' because usually they have been devised as protective practices.

† See *Equitable Payment* by Elliott Jaques (*op. cit.*) for an analysis of the nature of work.

crisis, they cannot be considered as the basis of a long-term wage policy.

3. *Wage determination by bodies of 'experts'.* Many proposals have been made based on the idea of using independent experts to settle disputes, to determine relative wages by job evaluation and, by one means or another, to determine what the national pattern of differentials ought to be.

But, however wise, just, expert, or independent, such bodies might be, I am quite certain that their establishment would not solve the problem of wage inflation. The reason is constitutional, as I have explained. Trade Unions have demonstrated time and again that they will not accept the right of external bodies to settle matters for them. The only bodies who have the experience to work out appropriate patterns of different wages and the power to impose them are the Trade Unions collectively. Groups of independent experts could go on making the most elegant proposals but if these were not acceptable to these power groups then they might as well not have been proposed at all.

Current confusion

These abortive attempts to tackle the problem of wage inflation display a state of confusion over the issue. I am convinced that the great majority of people of our country desire a situation where the level of wages earned reflects the level and importance of the responsibilities held and the work done. I believe furthermore that people have a shared and fairly consistent opinion about the order of importance of all the various occupations.* I am not suggesting that there is a highly detailed insight but that if the public were asked to put, in order of merit, machine operators, clerks, foremen, dock workers, policemen, teachers, managers, scientists, Civil Servants, doctors, railwaymen, engineers, and so on, a surprising consistency of attitude would emerge.

The public are becoming increasingly disturbed by a steady

* Recent research carried out by North Paul and Associates of 49 Queens Gate, London W2, appears to support this contention.

tendency for relative wages to be determined not by the importance of the work, but by the power of the Trade Union involved. For example, comparisons of the wages of Post Office, agricultural, and textile industrial workers, on the one hand, with those of dockers, printers, and car assembly workers, on the other, displays what are felt to be grossly unfair disparities – and yet those likely to achieve the most rapid rate of wage increase in the future are the latter rather than the former.*

In short, while I believe the country wants to start movement towards equitable differentials, the government are still relying on 'free bargaining' while the actual determinant of differentials is power.

Should employers play any part in the setting of national wage differentials?

When individual employers or federations of employers take part in negotiations with Trade Unions they are concerned almost exclusively with the viability of their own enterprise; those are the terms of their own employment. They do not take into account in resisting or accepting increases in wages and conditions, the level of earnings in their own concerns as compared to those in other industries and employment concerns.

Chief executives certainly have a large part to play in determining the differential wages *within* the employment hierarchies which they manage but they play no part in the setting of national wage differentials between industries.

Trade Unions, on the other hand, usually have members strung across a wide sector of the employment zone and intra-occupational differentials must be in their minds most of the time.

* There are even greater disparities if one considers company chairmen earning £50 000 p.a., land and housing speculators acquiring untold capital wealth and financial 'wizards' acquiring and selling companies. But as I have already stated, the means for dealing with these forms of unwarranted disparity in wealth are already available to a government which has the determination to use them. I do not therefore include them in my examples because I am attempting the description of a means of creating equitable wages, not of dealing with other forms of inequitable wealth.

Thus, recognition that the cost of labour no longer behaves like that of a commodity in the market, that free bargaining has become something of a myth, and that chief executives are not in a position to take into consideration national wage differentials, seems to me to remove any logical basis for employers to take any part in the process.

If, by the process that I shall presently describe, the task of working out and recommending differentiated national increases is carried out by Trade Unions, then employers would be required by law to implement them.

The idea that employers, while being excluded from the process of coming to conclusions about differential wage levels, should have to pay what was agreed will no doubt appear to be a very strange arrangement. But it emerges logically, I think, from the analysis which I have presented.

The effect of excluding them and leaving the argument to be conducted between Trade Unions is to introduce the necessary countervailing power to that of individual Trade Unions. They are brought face to face with each other and must be placed in a situation where, within limits set by Parliament, they have to agree on how differential wages of the various sectors of employment shall be adjusted. A new institution is required to achieve this.

The rules of procedure within such an institution should be those of 'Requisite Negotiation' which I have discussed already in Chapter 5.

No such institution has yet existed. No discussion between representatives of all occupations to obtain agreement about differential wages has been attempted nationally. This is what I refer to when I suggest that we lack an important national institution.

If a full package deal involving measures to keep prices in check, to deal with private exploitation of our resources, to contain excess profits, to prevent vast accumulations of private wealth, to curb the power of private wealth, and to make clear that abundant employment is impossible without control of wage inflation but is achievable on a permanent basis if excessive wage inflation is prevented, then it is possible that the Trade Unions might support the setting up of such an institution. I have drawn attention to the historical effect of power groups on the extension of the franchise. The involvement of Trade Unions in the working out of the pattern of differentials might persuade them to accept constitutional power in place of their power to disrupt.

I believe that Parliament must if necessary summon the resolution and courage to set up this new institution whether or not the Trade Unions accept the proposal. I am under no illusion as to the great difficulties which this would present. But there is no easy way out of the situation in which the nation finds itself. Great problems such as those which now exist in the employment zone cannot be solved by tinkering. They require substantial innovation. If the country has the imagination to realize that this is a constitutional problem and to realize how very desirable and important equitable wages and abundant employment are, then perhaps we shall acquire the determination to bring about the required changes.

In the next and final chapter I describe how the institution which I propose could work out in detail. Since I first attempted a description in pamphlet form some two years ago I have lectured more than forty times upon the subject to university and industrial audiences. In the light of questions and criticisms made by many extremely well-informed people I have continuously modified my ideas. I believe that they are now in a form which would prove workable.

CHAPTER 8

A national council for the regulation of differential wages (NCRD)*

I apologize to my readers for the three somewhat pedantic paragraphs which follow but I have to establish the meaning which I attach to some common words in order to describe simply the new institution which I wish to see established.

There are many types of Trade Union and there are professional associations which often possess many of the characteristics of Trade Unions. For the sake of both clarity and brevity I shall refer to both as Trade Unions.

There are many types of employing organizations such as industrial companies, nationalized corporations, commercial companies, social services, and so on. According to the function which they perform these employing organizations can be categorized into *employment groups* such as engineering, chemical, furniture, Civil Service, teaching, railways, banks, and so on.

Within the NCRD (National Council for the Regulation of Differential Wages) people in their role as members and representatives of Trade Unions will collectively decide the pattern of wage differentials to be applied to the same people in their second roles as employees of the different employment hierarchies which constitute each Employment Group.

Composition of the NCRD

Every type of occupation or professional association which was not already organized as a Trade Union and which wished to take part in setting the pattern of national wage differentials would have to form one.

The NCRD would consist, I suggest, of up to three hundred

* I continue to use the term wages to refer to the wages and salaries of all employed persons whatever their position and the term labour to all types of employee role.

members elected by the Trade Unions. Smaller Trade Unions would have to combine together simply for the purpose of sharing a single representative on the Council to look after their interests. Members of the Council would be paid a salary appropriate to being available on a full-time basis all the year.

The Council would be provided by Parliament with an independent chairman, a staff of research workers, and advisers with experience in Trade Union, commercial and industrial affairs. There would be no representatives of employers on the Council.

The great economic debate

Each year the government, after consulting with the National Economic Development Council and after debate and decision in Parliament, would announce the percentage amount which could be added to the national wage bill for the following year.

This, in fact, is the great economic debate which ought to take place in the House of Commons each year but which does not occur. Its subject, the division of our Gross National Product (GNP) between employees and all other demands upon it is of crucial importance. But to settle a great issue like this, as we do at present, in a series of fragmented wage battles between employers and employees, while others, who have the deepest possible interest in the outcome, take no part, is absurd.

The great issues upon which the political parties divide concern the relative proportions of GNP which are allotted to wages, unearned incomes, profits, capital gains, investment, social service, defence, education, supplementary benefits, pensions, and the like. But Parliament always has to leave wages out of the debate. The best that can be done at present is to debate financial provisions for the other issues on the basis of guesswork as to what will happen to the National Wage Bill during the ensuing year; and the guesses about wages have usually proved inaccurate in the past.

Parliament cannot be told by how much the National Wage Bill will increase and what share of GNP it will take because wages remain, ostensibly, the subject of thousands of 'Free Bargaining' sessions between employment groups and Trade Unions which will take place in the year to come. The Parliamentary debates and the government decisions about other financial matters are therefore to some extent unreal. Money alterations to the rate of government expenditure or taxation, or pensions, social benefits, and subsidies, have no precise meaning in terms of purchasing power until the rate of rise of the National Wage Bill is known with reasonable accuracy. If wages expand by twelve per cent instead of by a vaguely prophesied six per cent, bringing in their train general inflation, then a six per cent rise in social benefits for the poor may in the event be insufficient even to maintain the benefits at the real value of the previous prevailing rate.

I believe that the more politically minded of our Trade Union leaders have two aims in mind during wage negotiations. They seek increased earnings for their own members; but they also know that over the past century the share of our Gross National Product which has gone to employees as a whole has remained obstinately stable. They are attempting to increase that share via wage negotiations.

But thousands of unco-ordinated negotiations tend to produce general inflation which in the long run worsens the lot of the employee and the poorer sections of the community. They have no hedge against inflation like those who own investments or property. It is the latter who benefit from inflation.

Thus the logic of the situation is, I suggest, that the decision whether or not the employees' share of GNP should be increased is one which ought morally to be made by Parliament. It is certainly a decision which Parliament alone can make effective.

Function of the NCRD

The function of the Council (NCRD) would be to make recommendations to the government about differential percentage increases for the employees in different employment groups for the following year. These recommendations which would in total have to conform to the total percentage limit established in the 'Great Debate' would take the form of a specific, but probably different, percentage increase for each employment group.

Parliament might decide that the overall addition to the

National Wage Bill was to be six per cent. The NCRD proposals to Parliament might, for example, be four per cent to all those employed in the Engineering Employment Group, one per cent to the Ports Group, three per cent to the Civil Service Group, nine per cent to the Teaching Group, and so on.* The effect would be that every employer in a particular Group would be required to add to the existing wage of each of his employees the percentage appropriate to the Group to which his organization belongs.

Requisite Negotiation in the NCRD

In Chapter 5 I have described what I mean by the term, Requisite Negotiation. It involves unanimous voting on the part of all representatives of different associations of people coming together who have, somehow, to reach agreement.

This is a key factor in my plan whereby Trade Union representatives coming together in the NCRD will arrive at recommendations as to how the total addition to the National Wage Bill agreed by Parliament shall be divided up between all the different employment groups.

Unanimous voting is equivalent to the granting to every Trade Union representative on the NCRD of the right to veto the propositions put forward by others. It ensures that the strong cannot override the weak and it prevents majorities imposing their will on minorities. Most people will dismiss this manner of coming to decision as hopelessly idealistic – but on the other hand most people are quite unaware of the extent to which unanimous voting is currently in use. I have given many examples in Chapter 5.

The question is 'will it work?' and the answer cannot be certain. It is a matter of risk-taking as is always the case with constitutional change. The doleful prophecies of nineteenth-century statesmen about the results of extending the Parliamentary franchise did not prevent the passing of the Reform Acts. Those same statesmen gradually came to the conclusion that they had no alternative.

* There would be nothing to prevent the NCRD deciding to recommend specific money increases to the different employment groups instead of percentages if they so chose.

The details of the NCRD which I am proposing are merely illustrative but in principle I do not think we have any more choice today than our statesmen had in the nineteenth century.

The NCRD will be debating various plans prepared for them by their secretariat. They have a year to arrive at their recommendations. *If, at the end of the year they are still in disagreement then wages will remain frozen until they do agree.* Their debates will be in the full glare of publicity. Members of the NCRD who might be prepared irresponsibly to veto every plan which failed to provide for those they represent the full amount they felt to be their right would have to face not only other members of the Council but also reactions of the entire employed population. If their arguments are selfish they will be seen by all to be attempting to better the lot of one sector unjustifiably at the expense of the others. The country will begin to realize that what goes on in the NCRD is not the age-old tussle between employer and employee but a new kind of argument between employees. There will be no employers' representatives in the NCRD.

Another phrase one might use in referring to unanimous voting institutions is 'power-equating councils'. That is what they are. If every representative can veto the proposal of every other, then all have equal constitutional power. This situation forces representatives to debate and to face the necessity of compromise. By placing power groups together within such a constitution one produces the countervailing power to that of individual Trade Unions which is lacking in society today. Furthermore it is consistent with the democratic instincts of our country that representatives of all employees should alone formulate the recommendations which will lead to the law which impinges on these same employees.*

I think it is likely that, in the long run we shall have only two choices. We will have to accept either increasingly disruptive use of power or constitutional methods based on unanimous

---

* I feel it necessary to remind my readers constantly that my proposals are part of a package deal. The other parts, which are simpler to devise in principle, will deprive other lesser power groups of power to affect the living standards of others.

voting for settling the economic issues in the employment zone.*

Method of debate in the NCRD

The House of Commons is a majority-voting committee by constitution and has a culture of its own. On the various stages of a Bill or a general debate motions are put, debate takes place within a limited time programme, the vote is taken and the matter decided. It cannot be reopened the following week. It is too easy to fall into the trap of projecting these ideas on to unanimous-voting institutions.

I have seen unanimous-voting councils in action, dealing with crucial issues in industry over a period of thirty years. A motion is put, debate takes place, a straw vote is taken to discover the state of opinion, unanimous agreement is lacking, the debate continues, compromises are made, there is still insufficient agreement. The session closes, informal debate continues among the members of the council, shifts of attitude and further compromises and bargains are tentatively discussed. The next session opens and so the process continues.

The NCRD would have an immense task in front of them – namely dividing up the wage increase cake agreed upon in Parliament – but would have a year in which to complete the task. If by the end of the year they have failed to agree, then they carry on the debate. But pressure on them to make further compromise would be mounting, because as long as they continued to debate, wages of all would remain frozen.

* In previous writings about the NCRD I have proposed that at any rate in the early stages of the council the unanimous voting principle might be relaxed and that agreement would be by, say, ninety-five per cent majority vote. This would allow agreement notwithstanding the pressure in the Council of some representatives dedicated to its destruction. I now find myself uncertain whether or not this would be a necessary provision. If the Council's constitution made it possible for a Trade Union to withdraw its representative during a session, then a 'wrecker' could be replaced by another representative. I now believe that such a provision would make the relaxation of the unanimous voting rule unnecessary.

The relation of the NCRD to the government

The recommendations of the NCRD would be to the government. If accepted, the government would present a Bill to Parliament making the recommendations law. If the government decided not to accept the NCRD recommendations (very unlikely) it would send them back with its reasoned criticisms, for amendment by the NCRD. But the government could not amend the recommendations, because a single employment group which was deprived of a wage benefit by a government amendment of something which had been unanimously agreed by the NCRD would unquestionably be regarded by all as having been unjustly treated.

Sanctions to support inter-employment group differentials

The Wage Differential Act which implemented the NCRD recommendations would provide legal sanctions against those taking strike action in support of a wage increase in excess of what, by the Act, had become the legal pattern of differential wage increases for that year. The use of such sanctions would be restricted to action against the Wage Differential Act.

The form of sanctions would make it illegal for an employer, a Trade Union or any government agency to pay money to anyone on strike until he returned to work or resigned from his job and found employment elsewhere. This would not be difficult if full employment existed.

So long as 'Free Bargaining' between employer and Trade Union is the assumed basis of settling wage levels and so long as other interests in society are free to continue exploitation, then the use of sanctions against strikers is *immoral*. A government cannot be allowed to use sanctions against one side in a 'Free Bargaining' process. But in the new situation which I propose, a strike in defiance of the Wage Differential Act is not part of a battle over wages with an employer but a challenge to a national decision arrived at by a democratic process. *It is the rejection of the Market Theory of Wages, leading to the elimination of employers from the process of settling inter-employment-group differentials which changes the frame of reference and legitimizes the use of sanctions.*

Deprivation of all income including social support from government sources certainly sounds Draconic. But the purpose of the NCRD is to bring about a situation where the country can escape from the horrors of unemployment. If abundant employment exists then men are not driven to accept specific employment under the wage conditions brought about by the NCRD. They can obtain alternative employment if they find conditions in their current employment unacceptable.

In fact, I believe the threat of loss of all income would inhibit the strikes against the Wage Differential Law.* In the presence of such sanctions everybody would know in advance that there was no possibility of forcing a government to change the law. The strike would in fact be an attempt by the employees of one employment group or of one sector of an employment group to increase their wages at the expense of the employees of some other group.

Categorization into 'employment groups'

It would be necessary for every enterprise which employed people to be categorized as belonging to one or other employment group – for example, to the Engineering, Chemical, Agricultural, Mining, Teaching, Hospital Service, or Civil Service Group. Probably some subdivisions of such groups would be necessary. The task of deciding to which group different companies belonged would be difficult and would call for research, but the Department of Employment (and its predecessors) has for many years used such categories for the purpose of analysis of earnings, and other Departments already categorize employment into groups.

This may all sound somewhat bureaucratic but it has to be realized that a jungle of categories of a non-explicit character and of extraordinary complexity already exists. It would, for example, be almost impossible, at present, to write a comprehensible

---

* During the eighteen months' wage freeze initiated by the 1965–70 Labour government restricting wage increases to three per cent, no prosecutions were instituted for breaking this law.

account of how a single wage bargain between a Trade Union and an Employers' Federation in fact gets translated into wage adjustments for the individual employees whom it affects. If what I propose is regarded as a jungle of bureaucracy, I suspect that it would be a much more orderly and simple jungle than the one we exist in now.

Implementation of the Wage Differential Law

The percentage additions established by the Wage Differential Act would not apply to the members of particular Trade Unions or professions or types of occupations but to all those in individual employment groups. I have found in explaining this aspect of the working of the NCRD to others, that my proposals are frequently misunderstood. I therefore set out in Figure 10 a diagram which may help understanding.

On the left-hand side of the diagram appear the Trade Unions which represent people in their differing craft, occupational, and professional roles. A Trade Union does not normally represent all the employees of a particular employment hierarchy: different Trade Unions represent different types of occupations within the hierarchy. These are the representatives who decide, as members of the NCRD, what differential percentage wage increases will be granted to all the employees within each of the employment groups (on the right-hand side) which are themselves composed of employment hierarchies.

If the NCRD recommend and the government accepts, say, that the Engineering Employment Group are to receive five per cent, then that means that every person employed in every engineering company (so categorized) from chief executive to craftsman will have his existing wage increased that year by five per cent.* It would be obligatory on employers to pay that increase of five per cent by law.

* For the sake of simplicity I have not proposed as examples differentiated percentages for groups. But, for instance, it would be possible for the NCRD to recommend five per cent for those earning up to £x per week, four per cent for those up to £y per week and three per cent for those over £y per week within, say, the Engineering Group. (*Footnote continues on p. 95.*)

Parliament decides each year in a total economic debate the amount by which the total National Wage bill should be increased, say 6%

NCRD recommends to the Government the split up of the 6% between the Employment Groups

Government presents a Bill to Parliament which if passed makes the NCRD recommendations law for Employment Groups

NCRD

| Transport and General Workers Union |
| Civil Service Union |
| Railway Workers Unions |
| Teachers Unions |
| Engineers Unions |
| Managers Union |
| Agricultural Workers Unions |
| Miners Unions |
| ASTMS |

and so on

EMPLOYMENT GROUPS
pay the designated % to every employee

?	
4%	Engineering Companies
10%	Teaching Service
7%	Railway Industry
12%	Agricultural Industry
8%	Health Service
3%	Chemical Companies
6%	Retailing Industry
4%	Transport Industry
0%	Printing Industry

and so on

It has been pointed out as an objection to the foregoing general scheme that it would result, for example, in draughtsmen who are employed in many different types of employment group receiving different annual increases according to which group employed them.

At first sight this may appear to be a defect of my proposals but consideration will, I think, show that this is not so. In the first place, it is clear that draughtsmen (they are only an example of many different professions) are not paid at a uniform rate whatever type of hierarchy employs them. Secondly, the level of importance of work of draughtsmen will vary greatly from one employment group to another as well as within the same employment hierarchy. It is in fact not possible to make out a logical case for attempting to bring about a situation where all doctors, teachers, managers, craftsmen, etc., either receive the same wage or the same annual increment to those wages regardless of the employment group in which they work.

How long will it take the NCRD to bring about a situation where equitable wage levels for all would prevail?

Clearly, the degree of differential adjustment to inter-employment-group wages which could be made in one year would be small. If, for example, one were to postulate that teachers were felt to be underpaid by twenty-five per cent compared to others then it might take many years of over-average awards to correct this situation. If it were postulated that the Printing Group were overpaid, relative to others, by twenty per cent, then again it might take many years to bring about relative deflation of their wages by granting nil or under-average awards.

Equitable payment is a psychological situation where differentials are felt to be fair – not a mathematically factual situation. The important change which the employment zone requires is consciousness of movement towards a more equitable situation

---

In principle, the NCRD would be in a position to recommend any differential awards it chose. The Council would also have to take into account working hours, holidays, and fringe benefits, otherwise power bargaining would develop over these issues instead of over money wages.

rather than away from that situation as they appear to be doing today under the influence of power-negotiation.

Differential wages within employment hierarchies

The task of the NCRD would be confined to that of dealing with inter-employment-group differentials. But the internal differentials within employment hierarchies are equally important. A means must exist whereby dynamic adjustment of these internal differentials takes account of the continuous changes in the level of work being carried out by working groups and by individuals.

In fact these internal differentials are those which have always been under close and constant scrutiny by representatives of employees and managers. In contrast to the impossibility of the chief executive of a company being able, during wage negotiations, to take account of inter-employment-group differentials, such a person can and does bring into consideration wage relativities between different roles in the hierarchy which is under his managerial control.

Thus, my proposal is that internal differentials within hierarchies should be governed by negotiation between representatives and managers as is the case at present.*

An immediate objection to this procedure may arise with many people who will say that though the establishment of the NCRD has excluded power negotiation from inter-group differentials, such power negotiations will become rampant in relation to the negotiation of internal differentials. This, however, would not be so, because the sanctions embodied in the Differential Wage Act would operate against those who used strike action in an attempt to *force* management to pay wage increases in excess of the percentages specified for each employment group in the Act.

---

* Though it is possible to establish a situation where representatives of every stratum and type of employee within a hierarchy should by unanimous vote recommend to management the differential adjustments to wages which should be made. I have described such a system in Chapter 22 of *Organization* (*op. cit.*). It has been in operation for twenty years in one company, with success.

Negotiations over differentials within employment hierarchies would therefore be different from those which take place currently. They would not be overshadowed by threats of strike action. Internal differential wage adjustments would take place only when management and representatives of employees arrived at agreement.

It has been suggested that giving management the right to negotiate differential internal wage increases in excess of the percentages specified in the Differential Wage Act would lead to wage creep throughout the employment zone which would cause the Parliamentary decision on the total allowed addition to the National Wage Bill to be so far exceeded as to destroy the whole purpose of setting up the NCRD.

But I do not think that this is a real danger. The availability of sanctions against strikes which attempted to force employers' hands would profoundly alter the situation. I very much doubt if employers, released from the constant pressure of strike action, would irresponsibly agree large-scale increases. I do not believe that large employers would agree to such increases except for the rectification of what was felt to be differential unfairness within the hierarchies which they managed. The irresponsible minority would not be able to increase their prices if price controls were in operation.

Other commentators have suggested that in the presence of full employment many expanding companies searching for additional employees would seek to attract them by rapidly increasing their wage levels. Critics cite the case of the motor industry where this apparently happened during the twenty years after the war. But I question whether the wage increases in that industry were fundamentally due to shortage of supply of labour. I believe that they were more due to power bargaining by the shop stewards in that industry. Many economic writers in discussing wage inflation take too narrow a view of its causes and fail to consider appropriately the immense influence of strikes and threats of strikes in industries which fear to see huge amounts of capital invested in plant lying idle.

However, if I were proved wrong in the event it would be possible to correct the situation. A legally enforceable limit could be placed on the total amount which any management could voluntarily add to their own wage bill. It would be a small figure expressed as, say, one per cent of the total wage bill of the hierarchy. I do not advocate such a move in the first place because there would be the danger that it might come to be looked upon as the right of every employee to receive it. If it were all 'used up' in this way simply to increase the wages of every employee by one per cent, then there would be no scope left for attention to internal differentials.

Could these proposals bankrupt some companies?

It has been suggested by critics of my proposals that as employers would play no part in setting the new pattern of inter-employment-group differential wages, then the NCRD recommendations might include large increases of wages such as to render some industry uneconomic. This would hardly be possible. If we assume that the government limit on total increase of the National Wage Bill were to be six per cent then it is possible that the NCRD would recommend, say, twenty per cent to one employment group, but if it did so it would certainly have to be one which was in their estimation severely underpaid. It would be virtually impossible for the NCRD to agree to an increase of such a size for an already well-paid employment group. In addition, it has to be remembered that any increase above the six per cent has to be balanced by a weighted award to other groups of less than six per cent in order that the total new pattern of wages conformed to an average of six per cent. The foregoing possibilities need to be compared to what can happen under current conditions, where an award of twenty per cent or more is perfectly possible in industries where wages are already excessive in relation to others.

The changes of circumstances which would be brought about by these proposals

I am convinced that the improvement in the industrial situation brought about by putting these proposals into practice would be dramatic. Employers would be released from the continuous threat of disruption over wage claims. But they would have the new problem of attracting and retaining the services of their employees in the presence of abundant employment. This would be a most powerful stimulus not only to the investment of additional capital in order to save labour but also to the introduction of the many reforms which are required to make daily work the satisfying experience which it ought to be.

Industrial Trade Unions would have lost the power to increase the earnings of their members by unilateral action. But collectively, Trade Unions would have gained constitutional authority to set the National pattern of differential earnings. Parliament would have gained control over the division of gross national product between all sectors of society.

The package deal, which I have not spelt out in detail, accompanying the establishment of the NCRD would have committed the nation to the elimination of the grosser forms of inequality in wealth. The scene would thus have been set for a movement towards equitable wages and salaries, improved conditions of work and rising standards of living brought about by abundant employment.

The foregoing might prove to be excessively optimistic. But who knows? At least these proposals aim high and surely that is precisely what is missing today. We are dismally lacking specific initiatives which provide hope for the future.

Is this plan to control inflation a restriction on individual liberty?

Yes, it is. But though it is a serious restriction on the right of the individual to strike over wages it removes the much greater restriction on individual liberty brought about by the existence of unemployment.

Unsuccessful hunting day after day for the type of job you have done, and are suited to do, can produce in most people a feeling of the deepest depression and anger because they are robbed of the liberty to maintain themselves and their families by their own efforts. It deprives them of the liberty of choice of occupation. It may force them to accept employment of a kind which does not use their talents, which demeans them in their own eyes and forces them to impose a lowered standard of living on their families. I need not continue. Some sections of the population have suffered that fate for many years, and far too many other people, who up till now had no fear of ever being in that position, have in the last few years had to suffer in the same way.

We shall not escape imposing that kind of suffering on many people unless we are prepared to sacrifice some lesser liberties in order to achieve the greater ones. As Professor B. C. Roberts of the London School of Economics said in a recent paper written for an international symposium, 'The only condition under which unrestrained collective bargaining can flourish without causing damaging conflict and inflation is massive unemployment. This is a social cost no society is any longer prepared to tolerate for any length of time. On any national judgement it is an absurd price to pay for a system of wage determination which suffers from so many other defeats.'

Conclusion

I have sought in this book to establish that all people in the role of employee have certain basic rights apart from those customarily contained in a contract of employment. These are the right of appeal against decisions by their manager, the right to participate in the formation of the policies which circumscribe the authority of managers, the right to work in a situation of abundant employment, and the right to equitable payment. We live in circumstances today where the material standards of living are rising while the psychological and sociological standards are falling. We shall not reverse the growth of dissatisfaction, frustration, and hostility in the employment zone unless we are prepared for reform. Such reform falls into two parts. The first could be carried out fairly simply by employers. It involves setting up within each employment hierarchy the institutions required to ensure right of appeal and participation. In the Appendix I have set out an example of the type of agreement which managers could submit for agreement to the representatives and Trade Unions involved.

The second part, concerned with abundant employment and equitable payment, is a matter for Parliament. Perhaps, following the pattern of Reform Acts of the nineteenth century which established Britain as the great example of a liberal democracy, the changes could be introduced as the twentieth-century Reform Act. I hope we shall not have to endure too much strife and suffering before we become convinced of its necessity.

There is a real danger that some government faced with a sudden growth in the intensity of these problems will, in panic, go to the country to seek re-election on the basis of a series of authoritarian measures in a blind attempt to achieve a solution. If the electorate backed such a programme, then society would divide into employees versus the rest.

Because of that danger it is essential that as many democratic measures as possible which offer hope of resolving the problems of the employment zone should be the subject of wide discussion. That is the way to build up a healthy climate of opinion and to counteract the danger.

APPENDIX

APPENDIX

An example of a procedural agreement

GENERAL PRINCIPLES

1 The management and employees have a common objective to ensure the continuance of the operations of the company in the development, manufacture, and marketing of its products and in ensuring the efficiency of those operations in the interests of employees, shareholders, and customers.

2 Management must possess authority to make decisions about the operation of the company but the bounds of that authority are limited by policies set by directors on behalf of shareholders, policies established in the contracts negotiated with customers, and policies agreed in negotiation between management and the representatives of employees.

   Thus management recognizes the power of employees to set limits to the extent of their decision-making authority while employees recognize that within those limits management have the authority continuously to make the decisions (subject to individual appeal) which are necessary for the efficient operation of the enterprise.

3 It is recognized that continuous changes in the policies bounding the decision-making authority of managers are inevitable and that where they affect the interests of employees they cannot be changed without the agreement of the repre-

104

sentatives of all who might be affected. Accordingly, a policy-making institution shall be established in the form of a company or area council,* composed of the chief executive and representatives of all strata of employees.

4 Effective agreement on policy changes requires that all members of a council shall individually possess the right to veto proposals from other members until such modifications have been made as to render them tolerable and that the *status quo* shall continue to operate until agreement is reached. It is recognized that if a manager or any representative threatens to use power in an attempt to force change upon others then such an act is a breach of the constitution established by this procedural agreement.

5 Employees shall have right of appeal to higher authority against their manager's decisions in order to ensure that the terms and spirit of agreed policies are appropriately interpreted.

6 Every employee shall have personal right of access to the manager who allocates work to him, has personal knowledge of his performance, and has the authority to make decisions about him, based on that knowledge.

NEGOTIATING PROCEDURE

Intention

1 The company and the employees agree that it is in their mutual interest to observe a Negotiating Procedure by which all issues arising between them can be resolved as speedily as possible.

* Experience suggests that negotiating bodies operate best when they contain representatives of employees working within the same geographical area. Where a company operates establishments in different areas it will be found necessary to establish an area rather than a company council. In such a case it would be the chief executive of that area rather than of the company who would sit as management member. Similarly when setting up appeal mechanisms it would be the area chief executive who would preside at the final stage.

2 Issues which affect one person only will be dealt with under the Appeal Procedure.

3 Issues which affect one section only and are not felt by other representatives to affect their sections, will be negotiated between management and the representative or representatives of that section.

4 General issues affecting all sections will be referred to the council.

5 Normal earnings will be paid to employees in respect of time spent in meeting management to resolve issues.

Procedure

1 EMPLOYEE REPRESENTATIVE/SECTION MANAGER

1.1 If the employees are not satisfied with the conditions in their section the representatives will raise the matter on behalf of their constituencies with the section manager.

1.2 The section manager concerned must meet the representative with the least possible delay and will use his best endeavours to resolve the issue, consulting with other members of management if he feels this to be necessary.

2 REPRESENTATIVE/HIGHER MANAGEMENT

2.1 In the event of the section manager being unable to reach agreement with the representative rapidly, he will refer it to a higher level of management and the negotiations will continue there.

2.2 If, at the beginning of the discussions between the section manager and the representative, the section manager realizes that the changes sought are outside his personal authority, then he will refer the question to a higher level of management.

3 COUNCIL

3.1 If discussions between the representatives and higher management fail to resolve the issue, then at the discretion of either representative or management the matter will be placed on the agenda of the next meeting of the council.

3.2 Issues which involve more than one section or which can affect all sections may, at any stage in the Negotiating Procedure, be referred to the council.

3.3 Should the issue in question require urgent consideration then either the representative or management may call for an extraordinary meeting of the council.

4 GROUP INDUSTRIAL RELATIONS MANAGER/TRADE UNION OFFICIAL

4.1 If at any stage of negotiation either party to the discussion feels that the presence of a personnel officer and/or a Trade Union official would assist in clarification of the issues, then he or they will be asked to attend the negotiations.

4.2 Should the most senior personnel manager feel that the issues under negotiation are of importance to other areas of the group, then he has the right to be present.

5 Management will refrain from agreeing changes with Trade Union officials without the presence of elected representatives of the employees who may be affected.

6 TRADE UNION REPRESENTATION

If the majority of members in a department vote a Union member as their representative and that representative wants an official of the Union to assist him in discussion with management, then management will meet that official.

7 The use of power or threat of use of power either by managers or representatives in an attempt to force through a proposition at any stage of the negotiation is a breach of this procedure.

APPEAL PROCEDURE

1 Every employee shall have right of appeal against any decision made by his immediate manager which:

(*a*) he believes to be an infringement of agreed policy,
   or
(*b*) he feels to be unjust in its effect on himself.

2   The manager hearing the appeal will be referred to as the Presiding Manager. The Presiding Manager will ensure before proceeding with an appeal hearing that the appellant has discussed his grievance with his manager before appealing.

The Presiding Manager will record in words agreed by the appellant and the defendant the nature of the decision in dispute and the redress sought.

The Presiding Manager will give his judgement in the presence of both the appellant and the defendant and will record it in writing.

3   Should it emerge during an appeal that the appellant is in fact seeking changes in existing policy rather than reversal of his manager's decision, then the Presiding Manager will discontinue the proceedings and advise the appellant of the appropriate channels through which to pursue his objective.

4   Right of appeal shall lapse unless the employee notifies his intention to appeal within three working days of first being informed by his manager of the decision against which he wishes to appeal.

If the lapse of time exceeds three days then right of appeal is at the discretion of management.

5   Managers shall be accountable for ensuring that successive stages of any appeal are heard with the minimum possible lapse of time. They should be heard in terms of hours and days rather than weeks.

6   The appellant is allowed and advised to have present at an appeal his representative to assist him in presentation of his case. Alternatively, the appellant is permitted to have present another employee from his department or section or his Trade Union official.

7   The appellant and defendant have the right to call witnesses. Such witnesses will leave the appeal hearing when they have given their evidence and answered questions.

8   When the appeal of an employee is upheld the manager whose decision has been set aside shall himself have right of appeal to the next higher level of management.

9   The Presiding Manager shall prevent criticism by those present at a hearing of other persons not present. If threats of any kind are made the Presiding Manager will suspend the hearing until such threats are withdrawn.

10 If appellant and defendant agree, the issue in dispute may, at any stage of an appeal, be taken for advice, but not for decision, to a personnel officer.

11 The most senior personnel officer or his nominee has the right to be present at any appeal hearing.

12 After the final appeal before the chief executive (of the company or the area as the case may be), if the appellant remains aggrieved he has the right to be heard by the committee of which his representative is a member. If a majority of that committee of representatives believe that injustice persists in the case of the appellant they have the right to discuss the matter with the chief executive.

13 If the appellant is appealing against dismissal under the provisions of Sections 23 to 51 of the Industrial Relations Act, 1971, he shall have the right of further appeal to an independent referee or tribunal.

    If this appeal procedure is the subject of an order designating it for the purpose of Section 31 of the Act then, in accordance with Section 31 (2) (e) the appellant will have the right of appeal to an external tribunal or independent referee if the majority referred to in paragraph 12 above support a resolution to the effect that the dismissal is unfair.

DISCIPLINARY PROCEDURE

1   *Intention*

Sanctions must be available to managers to assist them in ensuring that agreed procedures, rules, and instructions are adhered to by their immediate subordinates and to be able to deal with subordinates whose performance is inadequate.

2 *Sanctions*

The sanctions available to managers are as follows:

(*a*) To indicate to an immediate subordinate that he is losing opportunity for promotion or for increase of remuneration.

(*b*) To transfer an immediate subordinate to another role within his immediate command which involves different work in the hope that the subordinate will perform better.

(*c*) To have an immediate subordinate removed from his position (de-select) and made available to the personnel department as a possible candidate for other vacant roles within the organization.

(*d*) If a manager believes that a subordinate is guilty of conduct which is prejudicial to the safety of other persons or of equipment, to instruct him to leave the company's premises and to take such other steps, within the law, as will lessen such danger.

3 *Procedure*

(*a*) A manager who is critical of an immediate subordinate's performance or behaviour must take all reasonable steps to inform the subordinate, to discuss the situation with him, to give further training if he feels it appropriate and, in general, to give him time to improve his performance or conduct.

(*b*) If the foregoing does not produce improvement then the manager must give the subordinate a first formal warning which the manager must record in his presence.

(*c*) If performance or conduct continues to be so unsatisfactory that the manager decides that de-selection may be necessary, he will give his subordinate a warning in writing of his intentions to de-select if performance or conduct has not improved within a stated period, state details of his criticisms, and inform the representative of the written warning so given. The subordinate may, if he so wishes, have his representative present when this second warning is given. The written details of the warning will be removed from the employee's record after twelve months.

4   *Right of Appeal*

As with all managerial decisions, those listed in this section are subject to appeal.

THE REPRESENTATIVE SYSTEM

Intention

1   The company has need of employee representatives in order that they may be aware of the viewpoint of their employees in all sections and at all levels.

2   The company acknowledges its duty to recognize the position of representatives of its employees and to be available to meet them.

3   The company recognizes that employee representatives are elected to state the view of their constituents which may not necessarily coincide with the personal views of those acting in a representative role, and that representatives have the duty and right to express their constituents' views.

4   It is agreed that employee representatives, if they are to undertake their duties effectively, must be given time off from their normal duties in their role of employee. A request must be made by the employee representative to his immediate manager for permission to leave his job in order to attend to his representative business. Such a request may not be unreasonably refused.

5   Where the numbers employed in a particular area or stratum of employees justify, in the opinion of the management, further facilities for the chairman or secretary or convenor of a committee of representatives, these will be provided and may cover an office, telephone, notice boards, secretarial assistance, document copying facilities, and relief from some or all work periods.

6   THE REPRESENTATIVE SYSTEM is composed of constituents,

constituencies, elected representatives, and committees of representatives. Decisions as to the boundaries of different constituencies, methods of election of representatives, and the committees which they may form, are matters for employees to decide.

The efficient working of the company will be rendered more difficult if constituency boundaries fail to coincide as far as possible with the organizational structure which divides the company into departments, officers and functions. Management are therefore concerned about the structure of the representative system and shall be provided with opportunity to comment before any particular arrangement is adopted.

7   Management must know what the structure of the representative system is, and when they meet a person who claims to represent some particular group they have a right to assure themselves that he does so by virtue of an election properly conducted under formal and appropriate procedures.

8   Management would feel assured on paragraph 7 above if the following methods of election of representatives are operated.

ELECTION PROCEDURE

1   Where large numbers of constituents take part in an election process, if a single ballot is used alone a danger arises that the person or persons may be elected by a minority of constituents.

2   Accordingly, the following method will be used:

(a) Any constituent may nominate a candidate if he can find a seconder.

(b) The number of candidates submitted for election by ballot shall be twice the number of vacant representative roles to be filled, if that number of candidates is available.

(c) If the number of candidates nominated shall exceed the number required, then those candidates receiving the highest number of nominations shall go forward for election. The number of candidates shall be increased if necessary to include those tying for the last places.

(d) In the vote by ballot those candidates, up to the number to be elected, receiving the highest number of votes, shall be deemed elected.

(*e*) In the event of a tie those tying shall take part in a further vote by ballot.

3 All ballots will be secret and will take place during working hours. They will be conducted by existing representatives or, if none exist in a constituency, by a combination of representatives from the other constituencies and personnel officers.

4 Administrative assistance, nomination forms, voting papers, ballot boxes, etc., will be provided by management on request.

5 Representative committees may, subject to the agreement of management (which shall not be withheld unreasonably), invite officials of recognized Unions to visit the company's premises to scrutinize the conditions under which the elections are held.

6 Elected Representatives will assume office on the first day of the month following the ballot and will hold office for twelve months.

CONSTITUTION OF COMMITTEES OF REPRESENTATIVES

1 The committee shall be known as the . . . representative committee.

2 *Functions*

2.1 To co-ordinate the work of those who are elected by different constituencies to represent the same strata of employees or employees who are members of the same trade unions.

2.2 To decide the boundaries of constituencies and methods of election of representatives.

2.3 To organize and scrutinize the election of representatives and to organize elections to fill casual vacancies in constituencies.

113

2.4 To be accountable to employees generally for ensuring that representatives carry out their duties in a constitutional manner.

2.5 For co-ordinating the views of representatives in order to protect their interests and to be able to provide management with a general picture of the views of employees.

2.6 To act as a co-ordinated means of communication with relevant Trade Union officers.

2.7 To elect from the members of their committee persons to serve on the council.

2.8 To negotiate with management on matters affecting the employees whom they represent and to refer to the area council issues upon which agreement with management is not achieved.

3 The committee shall be composed of all duly elected representatives from all the constituencies for which the committee is accountable.

4 A majority of members of the committee shall constitute a quorum of any ordinary committee meeting.

5 The chairman and secretary shall be elected by the committee at its first meeting following the annual election of representatives. They will serve as committee members for twelve months subject to removal at any time from office if a resolution to this effect is supported by seventy-five per cent of the members of the committee.

6 The committee may instruct their council representatives upon the matters which they wish to have placed on the council agenda.

7 The committee shall normally meet at least once each month, and at a time which enables them to consider the agenda of the next council meeting.

8 Minutes of each committee meeting shall be kept by the secretary and approved at the following meeting of the committee, and shall be available to all members of constituencies coming within the ambit of the committee.

9 Proposals for amendment of this constitution shall be published to members of all the committee's constituencies

at least twenty-eight days before the committee meeting at which they will be considered. Amendments shall be dealt with at an extraordinary meeting of the committee at which a quorum will be seventy-five per cent of members of the committee. Amendments to this constitution will require the support of at least seventy-five per cent of those attending an extraordinary meeting of the committee.

10   When a committee is composed of representatives of a stratum of employees which contains members of a Trade Union or Trade Unions recognized by management, then that committee shall contain within its membership at least one representative who is a member of each recognized Trade Union. Each committee will have power to co-opt such Trade Union members in the event that the elected representatives do not include such Trade Union members.

COUNCIL CONSTITUTION

1   The Council shall be known as the . . . council.

2   *Scope*

The scope of discussions shall cover any reasonable subject but no alteration of conditions controlled by National Agreements between Trade Unions and employers shall be made without reference to the appropriate Trade Unions.

3   *Authority of the Council*

Every member of the council (including the management member) shall have the right of veto over motions before the council except for motions on procedures.

Each employee member of the council must be reasonably confident before he gives an affirmative vote to a resolution:

(*a*) that the broad consensus of opinion in the constituencies and committee which he represents will accept the result as being at least tolerable, and (*b*) that the results of passing the motion will not be inconsistent with the policies of any Trade Union which is recognized by the company and of which he is a member.

In order to give an affirmative vote to a resolution the management member of the council must be confident that he will be able to implement the results effectively and that the resolution is consistent with his terms of reference from higher managerial authority from within the company. In the case of a managing director of a company he will have, before voting affirmatively on a council resolution, to be confident that the outcome will be consistent with his terms of reference from the board of directors and will not put at risk the relation of the company to its customers nor be inconsistent with contracts negotiated with them nor be inconsistent with the law.

4   *Functions*

4.1   To decide the policies within which management will have full authority to make decisions in operating the organization.

4.2   To revise, clarify or change old policies.

4.3   To establish a written code of policies covering all conditions of work.

4.4   To consider any matters placed on the council agenda in due form by members of the council.

4.5   To receive from the management member at its ordinary meetings a report on the affairs of the organization including such matters as market demand, forward load of work, organizational change, new plant or buildings, new products or new markets under consideration, where such matters can, in the opinion of the management member, be discussed without endangering the competitive future of the company or infringing the rights of shareholders.

4.6   To resolve disputes arising within the organization concerning conditions of work of employees.

4.7 To negotiate and decide upon differential grades and brackets of wages and salaries and other entitlements as between all strata, departments, and occupations of employees.

4.8 To refer for discussion and negotiation between management and representative committees or individual representatives matters raised before the council which are not of sufficiently *general* concern to warrant discussion by the council and which seem capable of resolution at lower levels of the organization.

5 Composition

The council shall consist of . . . members, all of whom shall be employees of the company, as follows:

(*a*) The management member who shall be the chief executive of the company or of the area, or his nominee.
(*b*) . . . members of the . . . representative committee.
(*c*) . . . members of the . . . representative committee.
(*d*) . . . members of the . . . representative committee.
(*e*) . . . members of the . . . representative committee.

6 Quorum

A quorum of the council shall consist of the management member or his nominee, and a majority of the members elected by each constituent committee of the council who shall include at least one member of each Trade Union recognized by management.

7 Officers of the Council

7.1 CHAIRMAN
The chairman shall be elected by the council from employees of the company at the first meeting of the council following the annual election of its members. To become duly elected the successful nomination must

have the support of a majority of representative members of the council and of the management member. The chairman shall not have power to vote.

If an elected member of the council be elected as chairman he shall vacate his voting place on the council and the appropriate committee shall elect another member in his place.

In the event of the management member being elected to the chair he shall retain his vote.

The chairman shall hold office for one year from the date of his election, shall be eligible for re-election, and shall be an ex-officio member of the council for four months after another chairman has been elected in order to assist the new chairman with his duties.

7.2 VICE-CHAIRMAN

A vice-chairman shall be elected by the council from among its members. He shall have the power to vote and in the absence of the chairman will take the chair with the powers set out in section 8 below.

7.3 SECRETARY

A secretary to the council and to the council's steering committee shall be elected by the same procedure as for the chairman. He shall hold office for two years. He shall not be an elected representative of any constituency during his term of office as secretary.

The secretary shall not be a member of the council but shall attend every council meeting and meetings of the council's steering committee.

When vacating office at the expiry of his term he shall, unless the council decides otherwise, have a duty to make himself available to attend at council meetings, and otherwise to assist the newly-elected secretary during the first two months of the term of office of the latter.

7.4 STEERING COMMITTEE

The steering committee of the council shall consist of the chairman (who shall have no vote) and one member of council drawn from each of the constituent representative committees of council and a nominee of the management member of council.

The function of the steering committee shall be to take such action on behalf of the council between meetings as shall be necessary. Decisions of the steering committee shall be by majority vote of its members but such decisions shall be subject to ratification by the council.*

The council, by resolution, may charge the steering committee with accountability for carrying out studies of situations, production of reports for council, and other such duties.

8 Procedure at Council Meetings

8.1 VOTING

There shall be two types of voting procedure:

(a) Unanimous voting which is required on policy decisions. This creates the power of veto.
(b) Majority voting on matters of council procedure.

The power to decide when a matter is one of council procedure shall be vested in the chairman, who shall rule before a vote is taken.

8.2 Any employee of the organization may attend as an observer at ordinary meetings of the council when they are held outside normal working hours. Those attending in this way shall remain silent. They may be removed at the decision of the chairman.

If in the opinion of the chairman or the management member of the council it would be detrimental to the

---

* Experience has shown that most decisions of such a steering committee are procedural rather than on matters of policy or principle.

interests of the company for the business of the council to be discussed in the presence of observers, such business shall be discussed in camera.

8.3 DEFEATED MOTIONS

If a substantive motion is defeated on a formal vote at the council meeting, further discussion shall not take place on that subject until a subsequent meeting of the council.

8.4 INDICATIVE VOTING

The chairman shall have power during discussion of a matter of policy to call for indicative votes to test the opinion of the council at any stage of the discussion.

9 Meetings

The council will normally meet once each calendar month and at the close of each meeting shall decide upon the date of its next meeting.

10 Extraordinary Meetings

The council chairman shall have power to convene and, at the request of the management member, shall convene a meeting of the council at any time.

11 Co-options to Council Meetings

11.1 The management member shall have power to co-opt other managerial personnel for advisory purposes and expedite business.

11.2 Members of council elected by any constituent committee of council may co-opt for any specific item one other employee of the company or an official of a trade union recognized by management.

11.3 Co-opted members shall not have power to vote.

12 *Power to Amend Constitution of the Council*

The council in meeting, subject to:

(*a*) the attendance of seventy-five per cent of its members,
(*b*) the giving of notice of the proposed amendment twenty-eight days before the meeting to the employees of the organization and to the local officials of the recognized trade unions,
(*c*) the resolution being subject to a unanimous vote,

shall have power to amend the constitution.

13 *Communication*

The agenda and minutes of council meetings shall be published without delay and be available to all employees of the company.

Policies formally decided by council shall be assembled suitably in loose-leaf books, copies of which will be held by all elected representatives, and will be available to employees in all departments and offices of the organization.

Bibliography

BROWN, WILFRED

'Principles of Organisation', *Monographs on Higher Management No. 5*, Manchester Municipal College of Technology, December 1946.

'Some Problems of a Factory', *Occasional Paper No. 2*, Institute of Personnel Management, London, 1952.

Exploration in Management, Heinemann Educational Books Limited, London; Southern Illinois University, Carbondale, Illinois, 1960; Penguin Books, Harmondsworth, Middlesex, England, 1965.

In Swedish translation – *Forskning l Företagsledning*, Strömberg, Stockholm.

In French translation – *Gestion Prospective de L'Entreprise*, Les Editions de la Baconnière, Neuchatel, Switzerland, 1964.

In German translation – *Unternehmensfuhring Als Forschungsobjekt*; Verlag W. Girardet, Essen, 1964.

In Dutch translation – *Nieuwe Wegen in Het Bedrijfsbeleid*, Spectrum.

In Spanish translation – *Dirreccion Empresarial*, U.T.E.H.A., Mexico.

'Selection and Appraisal of Management Personnel', *The Manager*, Vol. XXVIII, No. 6, 1960.

Piecework Abandoned, Heinemann Educational Books Limited, London, 1962.

'What is Work?', *Harvard Business Review*, September 1962; *Scientific Business*, August 1963.

'A Critique of some Current Ideas about Organisation', *California Management Review*, Fall (September) 1963.

'Judging the Performance of Subordinates', *Management International*, 1964, Vol. 4, No. 2.

Organization – Heinemann Educational Books Ltd, London, 1971.

BROWN, WILFRED, AND JAQUES, ELLIOTT

Product Analysis Pricing, Heinemann Educational Books Limited, London, 1964.

'The Business School Syllabus – A Systematic Approach', *The Manager*, April 1964.

Glacier Project Papers, Heinemann Educational Books Limited, London, 1965; Basic Books, New York, 1965.

BROWN, WILFRED, AND RAPHAEL, WINIFRED

Managers, Men and Morale, MacDonald and Evans, London, 1943.

HILL, J. M. M.

'A Consideration of Labour Turnover as the Resultant of a Quasi-Stationary Process', *Human Relations*, Vol. IV, No. 3, 1951.

'The Time-Span of Discretion in Job Analysis', *Tavistock Pamphlets No. 1*, Tavistock Publications, London, 1957.

'A Note on Time-Span and Economic Theory', *Human Relations*, Vol. XI, No. 4, 1958.

JAQUES, ELLIOTT

'Studies in the Social Development of an Industrial Community', *Human Relations*, Vol. III, No. 3, 1950.

The Changing Culture of a Factory, Tavistock Publications, London; Dryden Press, New York, 1951.

'On the Dynamics of Social Structure', *Human Relations*, Vol. VI, No. 1, 1953.

Measurement of Responsibility, Tavistock Publications, London; Harvard University Press, Cambridge, Mass., 1956.

'Fatigue and Lowered Morale Caused by Inadequate Executive Planning', *Royal Society of Health Journal*, Vol. 78, No. 5, 1958.

'An Objective Approach to Pay Differentials', *The New Scientist*, Vol. 4, No. 85, 1958.

'Standard Earning Progression Curves: A Technique for Examining Individual Progress in Work', *Human Relations*, Vol. XI, No. 2, 1958.

'Disturbances in the Capacity to Work', *International Journal of Psycho-Analysis*, Vol. XLI, 1960.

Equitable Payment, Heinemann Educational Books Limited, London; and Southern Illinois University Press, Carbondale, Illinois, 1961.

    And in French translation – *Rémunération Objective*, Editions Hommes et Techniques, Neuilly-sur-Seine, 1963.

'Objective Measures for Pay Differentials', *Harvard Business Review*, Jan.–Feb. 1962.

'A System for Income Equity', *New Society*, 12 December 1963.

'Economic Justice – by Law?', *The Twentieth Century*, Spring 1964.

'National Incomes Policy: A Democratic Plan', *Pamphlet Published by K.-H. Services Ltd.*, May 1964.

Time-Span Handbook, Heinemann Educational Books Limited, London, 1964.

    And in French translation – *Manuel d'Evaluation des Fonctions*, Editions Hommes et Techniques, Paris, 1965.

'Level-of-Work Measurement and Fair Payment: A Reply to Professor Beal's Comparison of Time-Span of Discretion and Job Evaluation', *California Management Review*, Summer 1964.

'Two Contributions to a General Theory of Organisation and Management', *Scientific Business*, August 1964.

'Social-Analysis and the Glacier Project', *Human Relations*, Vol. XVII, No. 4, November 1964.

'Too Many Mangement Levels', *California Management Review*, 1965.

In Preparation

BROWN, WILFRED
Exploration in Management, in Japanese and Italian translations.
Organization, in Italian translation.

JAQUES, ELLIOTT
Equitable Payment, in German, Italian and Spanish translations.

INDEX